D1058551

Who We Are

ELIZABETH MAY

REFLECTIONS
ON MY LIFE
AND CANADA

Who We Are

GREYSTONE BOOKS

Vancouver/Berkeley

To David, with thanks.
To Cate, my whole life.

14 15 16 17 18   5 4 3 2 1

Greystone Books Ltd.
www.greystonebooks.com

Cataloguing data available from Library and Archives Canada
ISBN 978-1-77164-031-2 (cloth)
ISBN 978-1-77164-032-9 (epub)

Editing by Nancy Flight
Copy editing by Maureen Nicholson
Jacket design by Ingrid Paulson
Text design by Nayeli Jimenez
Printed and bound in Canada by Friesens
Distributed in the U.S. by Publishers Group West

We gratefully acknowledge the financial support of the Canada Council for the Arts, the British Columbia Arts Council, the Province of British Columbia through the Book Publishing Tax Credit, and the Government of Canada through the Canada Book Fund for our publishing activities.

Greystone Books is committed to reducing the consumption of old-growth forests in the books it publishes. This book is one step toward that goal.

Contents

We stand now where two roads diverge. But unlike the roads in Robert Frost's familiar poem, they are not equally fair. The road we have long been traveling is deceptively easy, a smooth superhighway on which we progress with great speed, but at its end lies disaster. The other fork of the road—the one less traveled by—offers our last, our only chance to reach a destination that assures the preservation of the earth.

RACHEL CARSON, *Silent Spring*

Acknowledgements

THIS BOOK STARTED as a completely different book, which I was encouraged to begin by David Wynne. I am grateful beyond measure that when the book became a much more autobiographical work, because of the preferences of my publisher, David continued to offer invaluable guidance and assistance. My daughter, referred to throughout this book as Victoria Cate and now known just as Cate, was a very helpful reader. In the last rush to meet deadlines, her academic skills were invaluable in assembling and correcting endnotes and references. Many thanks to my friend, the brilliant Sarah Clift, for her sharp-eyed edits and improvements.

For many a childhood story, my brother's memory was a godsend in recalling details. Thank you, Geoffrey.

The sections dealing with climate science were reviewed and improved by Intergovernmental Panel on Climate Change (IPCC) authors, friends, and climate scientists Jim Bruce and Gordon McBean. My former partner and Cate's father, Ian Burton, an IPCC lead author, was, as ever, a great help. Jim MacNeill also reviewed drafts and verified the growth and evolution of environmental policy.

Dear friends Vicky Husband, Holly Dressel, and Debra Eindiguer helped in many ways to make this book a reality. Craig

Cantin from my Parliament Hill office, my Green Party executive assistant Jaymini Bhikha, and my constituency executive director Jonathan Dickie—time and again they gave critical support as I tried to squeeze in time to write.

My editor at Greystone, Nancy Flight, was patient and tolerant as I dug in my heels over many issues. The book is much improved by her efforts.

To my family, who have loved and supported me—Cate; my brother, Geoff; his wife, Rebecca-Lynne; my stepchildren, Nadya, Sasha, and Jo; their partners Gordon, Cristie, and Richard; and my seven grandchildren—Lonya, Misha, Dante, Hudson, Skye, Moss, and Nina Liv—I can never thank you enough.

WHY THIS BOOK?

T HIS BOOK IS about Canada, about who I am and who we are. It is about who we have become. Canada seems to have lost its sense of self. In the last number of years, the sense of who we thought we were has been shaken. We need to take stock and commit to being the best we are capable of being—as a people, as a nation.

This book is an argument for our future, the future of our children, and the future of our grandchildren and generations beyond.

It is about how diminished democracy undermines our best hope to avoid the worsening climate crisis, which threatens human civilization itself.

It is a book about how we can make a difference, about how we can and must take back our country and steer a course to benefit the many and not primarily to advantage the few. It is an argument for change. In this sense, it is a vision.

My vision is not drawn from any tract or ideology, but comes from paying attention throughout six decades of living. My perspective was formed through decades of bearing witness to the ways in which bad public policy causes the innocent to suffer and how good public policy can transform societies. My vision comes from an unusually political childhood, an activist upbringing, and a deep love of democracy. It comes from knowing that working together changes the world. It comes from a single mom's sense for problem-solving. It comes from being a member of parliament who understands that my "boss" is the people who elected me, not some backroom of political operatives.

Over my lifetime, I have witnessed the rise of corporate power and the shrinking of the public sphere, the commodification of everything and the dumbing down of society, and the degradation of every ounce of sacred creation, right down to our genetic material, into feedstock for the corporatist enterprise. As economist David Korten once put it, "This is no longer a clash between 'isms'... It is the choice between Life and Money."[1]

When the rapacious behaviour of transnationals is supported or ignored by government, we are endangered. When the positive and transformational power of corporate leadership is engaged for the public good, we are inspired.

I look back through time, through historical and political periods connected to my childhood, through the stories of my elders. This word-of-mouth link leaves me feeling connected to times before my birth, times like the Great Depression, the Second World War, the American Civil War, and even the American Revolution. My family remembers its history. I grew up in the United States, and three of my ancestors signed the Declaration of Independence. As a teenager, I moved to Canada and absorbed Canada's history, rewiring my brain to a Loyalist tradition.

My view of our role in the world is influenced by both my early years in the United States and my adult life in Canada, where I came to know and love my country with the intensity often found in new Canadians.

Perhaps Marshall McLuhan was right in observing that "Canada is the only country in the world that knows how to live without an identity." For many Canadians, "who we are" is defined by "who we aren't." We are not our closest neighbour.

Nevertheless, a unique Canadian identity shines through our ambiguities. The more Canadian I felt, the more I knew I was changing how I defined myself in more profound ways than slipping on a new set of clothes.

In 2003, when Bono said, "The world needs more Canada," it sounded right. We were the country other countries wanted to be.[2]

We thought we had earned our good reputation for leadership, for caring stewardship of a huge chunk of Planet Earth's forests and water, for compassionate policies at home and abroad, for being a bridge between North and South, a peacemaker and peacekeeper—a good neighbour. We loved that story about U.S. kids stitching Canadian flags to their backpacks to get a warmer welcome as they hitchhiked the globe. We even loved, with a Canadian capacity for self-deprecating humour, the winning entry in a *New Republic* "most boring headline" contest: "Worthwhile Canadian initiative."

It has become a habit to think we deserved our own good press. Nearer the truth, perhaps, is that it was, in many ways, undeserved. U.S. environmental law has always been stronger than ours. Our international development assistance has always lagged behind that of our European partners.

When looking at the military-industrial complex and foreign wars based on misguided policy and false flag events (that is, when governments create fictional events to justify wars), comparisons with the U.S. put us in a favourable light. We largely missed how many other countries around the world outperformed us in poverty alleviation, social justice, environmental protection, and the green-tech revolution. Whether we were riding on our natural good natures and welcoming culture or on the promotional efforts of our diplomats, we still managed to maintain our good reputation. Until now.

We have withdrawn from international treaties and institutions that address some of the world's most critical issues. We are no longer leading; we are not even following. We have quit cold. Is this the Canada we want to be in the world? Is this the Canada we want for our children?

Leadership comes not from spinning and misleading Canadians, leading us myopically down a fossil fuel–dependent road for the benefit of a few. It is not enhanced by spending millions on advertising that proselytizes economic growth and job creation linked to fossil fuels, ignoring that better and more sustainable jobs are created in clean tech, renewables, and energy conservation. Leadership comes from providing a renewed vision of an equitable and sustainable future and from creating a path to reach that common future.

Getting on that path requires being resourceful, pragmatic, creative, and innovative. We must mobilize technology, advance education, and provide, stimulate, and reward Canadians with the means to adapt, conserve, market internationally, and provide—not dismantle—sustainable frameworks for international cooperation.

While not given to bouts of jingoism and mindless patriotism, we are aware how deeply fortunate we are to live here, to be Canadian. Travel increases our sense of gratitude. To visit other countries is to realize how extraordinary it is to live in a place with a massive land mass and only 35 million people.

Yet, even if we know intellectually that our circumstances are unique—we are wealthy (for the most part), industrialized, and privileged, with huge tracts of wilderness and millions of lakes and rivers as well as vibrant, culturally diverse urban centres— day to day, it is easy to forget. It is easy to imagine that our state is the lot of most of humanity. That is the flip side of our luck; we are spoiled. We are wasteful.

We waste water, vying with the U.S. as a close second for per capita water consumption. We waste energy—we use more energy per person than Americans and more than half of the energy we use is wasted.

We send huge volumes of stuff to landfills, having swallowed whole the U.S. inventions of single-service items, drive-through windows, and "shop till you drop" as a statement of fun. This cultural shift, from our grandparents' notion of "waste not, want not" to shopping as entertainment was no accident. It came right out of the U.S. postwar cocktail of *Mad Men*, of television, advertising, and marketing.

In 1955, Victor Lebow set out his prophetic prescription for a consumer society in the *Journal of Retailing:*

> Our enormously productive economy demands that we make consumption our way of life, that we convert the buying and use of goods into rituals, that we seek our spiritual satisfactions, our ego satisfactions, in consumption. The measure of social status, of social acceptance, of prestige, is now to be found in our consumptive patterns...
>
> We need things consumed, burned up, worn out, replaced, and discarded at an ever-increasing pace.[3]

Canadians heeded the call. On solid waste, we are number one in the world. Not only is the green plastic garbage bag a Canadian invention, we create more solid waste per capita than even the usual number one in waste society, the U.S.

Yet we think we are more environmentally conscious than we are. We think we are green because we have a blue box on the curb, while the rate at which we waste water and create garbage has increased dramatically since the 1980s.

Canadians are not the only people to experience cognitive dissonance between how we see ourselves, our aspirations, and our behaviour and how we really are, but we may be among the world's most smug.

The advent of Stephen Harper and his visitation upon Canada of the policy equivalent of a plague of locusts was disturbing to a nice bunch of people like us. Harper's assault on Canadian criminal justice, immigration, refugee, science, statistics, foreign, and environmental policy was a shock.

We never knew we were not great environmentalists, so it has been a rude awakening to have a prime minister who makes no bones about it. We were sure the Charter of Rights and Freedoms and our progressive sense of fair play would preclude embracing failed criminal law policies, like mandatory minimum jail terms. We were sure that we valued our international reputation, so having a prime minister who rushes from the United Nations General Assembly, without bothering to give a scheduled address, for a photo op at Tim Hortons, is also unnerving.

In some ways, Stephen Harper may have done us a favour. We have been knocked out of complacency as he held up a mirror to our collective face, and taunted us with "This is what you really look like."

Since 2006, when Stephen Harper's Conservative Party first formed a minority government, I have imagined that Canada's identity crisis needed a self-help book called *When Bad Governments Happen to Good People*.

This is not that book.

This is a book about how I got to be what I am today. A Canadian leader of a federal political party who believes democracy would be improved if we had never invented political parties. A civil libertarian who knows that, if you are looking for justice, the legal system rarely delivers. A lawyer in recovery, aspiring theologian, feminist, vegetarian, writer, cook, sister, daughter, single mother, grandmother, campaigner, activist, citizen.

This is a book about how we got where we are today—a decent country of immense potential, suddenly on the wrong side of history. How a country with a well-educated and, for the most part, economically secure population ended up with a dwindling percentage of its citizens who bother to vote. How a parliamentary system could be so degraded that it now more resembles an elected dictatorship than a healthy democracy.

This is a book about how to fix what is wrong, rescue democracy from hyper-partisan politics, and put Canada, and the world, on the path to a secure, post-carbon economy.

We have a lot of the right stuff to make it work. But no politician is going to be adequate to the task. There is a leadership vacuum. I invite you—I invite all of us—to fill it.

A Family History That Is History

[The year was 1777.] It was while the British were in possession of Clover Hill that, one morning, two little children, one a girl of five, and the other a boy of four, were playing in the hall, and, impelled by youthful curiosity, they looked in at the door of what was called by the family "the north Parlor," to see the red coats. They saw them seated around the table drinking wine, and as Lord Cornwallis caught sight of the children, he called to the little boy to come and sit on his knee. According to the custom of the times, a toast was proposed, and Lord Cornwallis, presenting the child with a glass of wine, said: "We will give you a toast, my little fellow, and you shall have this glass of wine. Drink to the health of His Gracious Majesty, King George the Third." The glass was emptied by the little child in a moment. "And now, my little fellow," said Lord Cornwallis, "you shall name the next toast, and we shall drink to it. What shall it be?" Without a moment's hesitation, the child, standing on his feet, and holding his glass high, said, in a clear voice: "George Washington." Amid much applause at the bravery of the little child, the assembled company emptied their glasses, and Lord Cornwallis called him a brave little fellow and praised him for his independence. This little boy was my grandfather, Mr. Samuel Hazlehurst.

FROM A SPEECH THOMAS HAZLEHURST MIDDLETON, MY GRANDFATHER, DELIVERED TO THE COLONIAL DAMES OF AMERICA ABOUT HIS GRANDFATHER.

Chapter One

THE FORMING
OF AN ACTIVIST

I WAS BORN ON June 9, 1954. My mother told me she fed nickels into the radio attached to her bed in the Hartford Hospital to stay tuned to the Army-McCarthy hearings. Whether she intended it or not, this guaranteed that among the first sounds processed in my infant brain were political newscasts. The words that rang out like a death knell to Joseph R. McCarthy's reign of fear-mongering came across that radio that day: "Have you no sense of decency, sir?"[1]

A wooden angel was placed over my crib at home, but a mushroom cloud would have been more appropriate. The potential for mutually assured destruction was the constant nighttime companion of children of the Cold War fifties.

Our mother did her best to shield my brother and me from nuclear anxiety, keeping us home whenever the school asked parents to send kids to school with blankets and pillows to be used in practice drills for nuclear war. The "duck and cover" training seems absurd now, but the threat of nuclear war was real. We only found out about the Cuban Missile Crisis the day after it passed, when my parents seemed unnaturally happy to be alive.

My childhood was marked by my mother's campaigns against nuclear weapons testing. Her commitment to end the testing

9

of H-bombs in the atmosphere was a manifestation of maternal instinct. As a new mother, she was intensely aware of warnings from scientists that nuclear atmospheric testing was dispersing clouds of toxic radioactive fallout, which would accumulate in children's bones and increase the incidence of childhood leukemia. Although she tried to shield us from these facts, her concerns rubbed off on me. I warned the other children in kindergarten not to eat the snow because it contained strontium-90. This did not make me popular.

Because my parents wanted us to learn French, we were put in private school. But my mom's activism led the other parents to brand her a Communist, with the result that my little brother, Geoffrey, and I were rarely included in class parties and mostly ostracized in class. Geoffrey still describes our life from nursery school to grade nine, when we left Renbrook Country Day School, as being "prisoners of conscience."

In contrast to my mother, my father was by choice and by character a retiring man and preferred to stay in the background. Norman Cousins, then editor of the *Saturday Review*, a friend of my mother through her work against the bomb, and an adopted uncle to me, once introduced him as "Mr. Stephanie May." Being both unusually forgiving and proud of all my mom did, my father took it in stride. When Senator Eugene McCarthy finally met him, after years of knowing my mother and me, he greeted him with a cheery, "He lives!"

John May was no different from many fathers in the 1950s—a good provider working long hours in the corporate world of Insurance City. When I read James Thurber's "The Secret Life of Walter Mitty," I thought Thurber must have known him. In my father's spare time he escaped into military history, staging battles with battalions of toy soldiers. Every June 18, the Battle of Waterloo was refought with my brother and me and friends and neighbours commanding the troops in our backyard. We thought everyone knew that the anniversary date of the Battle of Waterloo was June 18, 1815.

10

My father had grown up in the UK of British parents but, by an accident of history, was born in the U.S. His father, a commercial artist and painter, was making a living in Manhattan in the 1920s when my father was born. Then, on a family visit to Barnet, England, the stock market crash forced them to stay. With no memory of the U.S., John grew up outside London and had an adolescence dominated by the blitz, buzz bombs, and the all-too-routine loss of his neighbours. Having served in the Home Guard, he found himself at the age of eighteen with the choice of joining either the British or the U.S. Army. He chose the U.S. Army, which gave him the postwar GI Bill and an education in accountancy at Columbia Business School in New York.

It was at Columbia that my parents met, as my mother pursued her talent as a sculptor at the Arts Students League, and he pursued accounting and her. After graduation, he took a job at Aetna Life and Casualty in Hartford, Connecticut. By then, my parents were married.

Years later, after President Kennedy signed the nuclear test ban treaty, my mother's campaigning moved on to marches, picnics, and church events in support of the civil rights movement. I remember great days in interracial softball games and summer schools where I helped kids from the inner city learn to read. Then, in January 1965, Lyndon Johnson (who had run for president on the promise that he would not send American boys to Vietnam to do what Vietnamese boys should be doing for themselves) started the aerial bombardment of North Vietnam. The rapidly escalating war in Southeast Asia, with its napalm and horror, remained the focus of our family life until we took a summer vacation to Cape Breton Island in 1972.

We fell head over heels in love with Cape Breton. It was perhaps the beauty and tranquility of Cape Breton, so far from the political angst and turmoil of the U.S., that led my parents to pack it all in and move there for good. They toyed with ideas for what they would do in their new life, as if discussing a new hobby. It

11

never occurred to them that such a move could wipe us out financially. With more determination than experience, they decided the future lay in running a restaurant.

We had never been a nomadic family. In Connecticut, we had lived in the same house on seven acres, with ponies, sheep, chickens, an extremely obstinate donkey, and an assorted menagerie, for eighteen years. The woods in back of our house were an almost inexhaustible place for adventure. I often think it was the closeness to nature I experienced as a child that made me an environmentalist.

It certainly had a lot to do with our lambs. The first impact of my mother's impetuous decision to give Geoffrey and me pet lambs as Easter presents was that, not so gradually, we became vegetarians. As we watched in joy while our lambs frolicked, my parents' friends, all too often, would make cringe-worthy comments such as "Be sure to invite me when lamb chops are on the menu." One family friend asked my brother, "If you aren't going to eat them, what are they for?" Despite the shock of the question, Geoffrey, at age eight, managed to answer, "They are for... to love."

Further testament to our innocence was that I never understood why my parents' friends laughed when I tried to remember the breed of our sheep. I would say, "They are Norfolks or Suffolks or some kind of fuck." They were, in fact, Suffolks, black faced with white wool.

When our lambs grew up, we sent them back to the flock to be bred in hopes of more lambs. Soon Smokey and Baaa gave birth to their own lambs. My grade six science project was a detailed chronicling of the gestation and birth of Corey (to Smokey) and Thunder and Spring (to Baaa). Raised outside of a flock, these new lambies of ours were amazing. They came when they were called, by name, as smart as any dogs we had ever had. Thunder and Spring were twins and their mother, Baaa, was the good mother, interested in educational opportunities, taking Thunder and Spring on long walks around the property. Smokey was not a great mother, refusing to nurse Corey and always looking for more grain. She stayed near the barn. Mama's boy Corey stuck to her like glue and that saved his life.

To wean them, the lambs were sent back to the farm where they had been purchased. While they were away, Baaa became horribly ill. She had convulsions, twitching and thrashing. I tried to soothe her in the back of our station wagon as my mother drove madly down the winding country roads to reach the vet. After Baaa died, my mom asked for an autopsy. No answers came. No toxic leaves in her stomach contents; no sign of how she could have died.

Her poor baby lambs came back after weaning and looked everywhere for their mother. Corey had Smokey, but Thunder and Spring searched in vain. We would see them on the lawn grazing, and suddenly they would look up at each other, bleat happily, and tear off toward some place they had just thought of and not yet searched. They would return dejected. It was excruciating to watch. Spring lost her voice from crying. Her bleat became a croaking incomplete "baaa." Worse was to come. First Thunder and then Spring developed the same symptoms as their mother. The harrowing trip to the vet was repeated twice. Their eyes rolled back in their heads and they frothed at the mouth, as I tried to tell them I loved them and they'd be okay.

Years later, in junior high school, I read Rachel Carson's *Silent Spring* and learned about pesticide poisoning of sheep in Arizona.[2] Rachel Carson could have been describing my own lambs. The symptoms of nervous system intoxication from pesticides exactly matched how my own sheep had died. These were a class of pesticides developed from the science of Nazi experiments with nerve gas. In large doses, they could kill people. In smaller doses, these inventions could be used in poisons to kill insects, but they were incidentally killing sheep, contaminating streams, poisoning eagles. And, as Rachel Carson suspected, compromising our own health.

13

I tried for a dispassionate calm as I composed my inquiry to the Town of Bloomfield, Connecticut, asking if it had any record of pesticide spraying in the months from May to July 1966. Yes, came the reply. Malathion and methoxychlor had been sprayed on the roadsides. All those nature walks Baaa took with the babies. All their searches for her in their usual haunts. I wrote back that the town spraying programs had killed our sheep. No reply came to that.

After reading *Silent Spring*, I started a file on pesticides. I joined Friends of the Earth and Sierra Club. I started subscribing to *Environment* magazine, published by the Scientists' Institute for Public Information.

When we moved, my parents decided the house would show better to potential buyers if we left it furnished. I left so many things I cared about behind, but I took my box of files on pesticides. And that is at least part of the reason that Cape Breton Island's forests were never sprayed. But that is a much longer story.

The summer we loved as tourists in Cape Breton was a far cry from the winters. I found the best way to force myself forward in a driving wind was by yelling "Heathcliff!" as I soldiered on. The word was snatched from my mouth, with a rush of air.

For the first few years, we lived in the one-room log cabin adjacent to our restaurant and gift shop. My father had decided we couldn't afford the heating costs of the house we owned on the other side of the island in Baddeck. As the cold wind blew across the pack ice on the wintry Gulf of St. Lawrence, the first thing it hit was us. Inadequately chinked, the gaps between the logs let snow blow into one corner of the cabin, where the inefficient barrel oil stove failed to generate enough heat to melt the snow in the far corner. The next winter, we wrapped the cabin in plastic. That helped somewhat, but not much.

14

I had a dream our second winter. Now that I was a waitress, and not a university student, I often dreamt of the summer season and serving tourists. In one such dream, a tourist looked out at the log cabin and asked why it was wrapped in plastic. My dream self answered, "To keep it fresh."

It was hard, but I loved the land and I loved being in Canada.

Sometimes, the best way to understand and appreciate something is to first see it from the outside.

For an American, Canada is easy to love—with a language and culture familiar to anyone who has grown up in the U.S., but sufficiently and fundamentally different in ways that set Canada apart.

For my Cape Breton neighbours, the time before the universal health care system was established—when people used to die from preventable illness, women died in childbirth, and poverty sent family members to early graves—was still within living memory. The health care system represented a fundamental difference between the place where I had grown up and the place where I would choose to live my adult life.

I still recall an oratory competition between the older kids in that dreaded Republican-dominated private school I attended in Connecticut. Crane Taylor had brought his fist down on the podium in a passionate three-minute rant against Medicare, spitting out, "And that, ladies and gentlemen, is socialism!" I went home and asked my mom what socialism was. If it meant universal health care, it certainly sounded like a good idea to me. And now I was living in a country where no "isms" were attached to health care. It simply ensured that people would not die for lack of money for medical care.

Because our life in Margaree Harbour, a village of forty-two people, was not the typical life of most Canadians in 1974, I largely experienced what it was to be Canadian through television. Our TV set, focal point of the one-room cabin, received exactly two channels—CBC and Radio-Canada. "He shoots! He scores!" in two languages.

CBC-TV was my introduction to life beyond Cape Breton. We loved that our new land was willing to ridicule its politicians. In the U.S., *The Smothers Brothers* was cancelled for allowing Canadian comic David Steinberg to deliver irreverent sermons, though it was generally accepted that it was Pete Seeger singing "Waist Deep in the Big Muddy, and the Big Fool Said to Push On" that really caused the show's demise. Pete Seeger made the "big fool" too obviously Lyndon Johnson and the swamp too clearly Vietnam.

In contrast, Canada boasted any number of satirical shows where nothing seemed off limits. They included *The Royal Canadian Air Farce*, *Up with Canada*, and talk shows where smart people like Paul Soles and Adrienne Clarkson engaged in witty repartee. Even the children's shows were smart. I became a fan of an unknown Dan Aykroyd playing a Glaswegian policeman on a show called *Dr. Zonk and the Zunkins*. TV was funnier and smarter than in the U.S.

The CBC evening news provided backgrounders on the issues at play in upcoming elections in other countries. It was a revelation—the newscast assumed Canadians were interested in what was happening in Italy or in Japan. Never in all my years of watching Walter Cronkite had I watched news like this. True, Canadians were much more likely to know a great deal more about U.S. politics than the latest developments in Belgium, but there was no chance the U.S. TV news would have provided the internationalist perspective we imbibed as Canadians.

I had loved reading de Tocqueville, and I imagined what he would say of the cultural personality differences between my old country and my new one. It seemed fitting that, where the U.S. Declaration of Independence stated that its purpose was to protect "life, liberty and the pursuit of happiness," Canada's formative document, the British North America Act, set out the workman-like goals of "peace, order and good government."

16   I had always been interested in politics, watching as my mom took up one losing cause after another. She had campaigned tirelessly for Adlai Stevenson and counted him among her friends. But it was Eugene McCarthy who was my first case of complete

and total hero worship. It was odd that he should have been my friend and correspondent before he was my mom's.

Following in my parents' interests, I had joined the United World Federalists in grade one. This led to occasionally getting mail from other worthy organizations. One such letter, from Senator Eugene McCarthy of Minnesota, urged progressive Americans to donate to the National Committee for an Effective Congress, ensuring scarce campaign donations went to those candidates who had the best chance of improving democracy anywhere in the U.S. I was in grade five by then and thought the whole proposition was very sensible. I sent the committee all I had in my bank account, saved from my allowance. My mom included that detail with the cheque she sent to the committee.

Senator McCarthy responded by mail, suggesting he would love to meet me if I should ever be in Washington. It was nearly the Easter break at school, and my mom decided it would be a good time to go to DC. As we sat in the senate dining room, Eugene McCarthy introduced my mom, my brother, and me to the senators whom I most admired for their opposition to the looming war in Vietnam—Albert Gore (father of Al), Wayne Morse, Mark Hatfield, William Fulbright—all of them asking where we lived in Minnesota. Connecticut? They said, "Gene, isn't that Tom Dodd's job?" And Senator McCarthy would say, "Well, Elizabeth is a special friend of mine."

No wonder that my mom and I were in Chicago in December 1967 for a historic event. Eugene McCarthy announced he would challenge a sitting president in a bid to end the war in Vietnam. And my mom organized and found a way to force town-by-town primaries in Connecticut, winning a delegate seat in the August 1968 Chicago Democratic National Convention. She brought me along so that I could see "democracy in action." It was a signifi- 17
cant part of the formation of my political consciousness. As one McCarthy delegate said of the experience, "I wasn't convicted and sent here. I was elected and sent here."

It is worth knowing that democracy is fragile. That police can riot, that you can get tear-gassed while watching sailboats on Lake Michigan, and that sometimes it is possible on a dark street in a scary neighbourhood, for your mother to squeeze your hand and say, "Don't worry. We'll be fine as long as we don't see a policeman."

My life can be demarcated in a number of ways, like slicing a knife through time, leaving one part so very different from the other that it might be an exercise in time travel. Or reincarnation. One life so different from the other that it is as though someone else has taken your place. In my case, one clear demarcation was in 1973, when I stopped being the privileged daughter of a well-to-do Connecticut family and became a waitress and cook in my family's seafood restaurant on the edge of the spectacular Cabot Trail on Cape Breton Island and on the edge of bankruptcy. My mother would occasionally suggest I had brought this misfortune on the family from reading too much Isaiah. I had not felt good about wealth, but I cannot say I enjoyed poverty. My mother mostly kept her sense of humour, describing us as *nouveau pauvre*.

She did feel terribly guilty that I couldn't afford to go to university. I had been planning from age thirteen to be an environmental lawyer. I had been in a hurry, gaining exemption from first-year university courses through advanced placement exams and wanting to be through Yale Law School by 1978. We had known so many bright Yale law students through our political campaigns for peace candidates, Bill Clinton and Hillary Rodham among them, that it seemed natural that I would be going there too. Bill Clinton had been asked by Senator George McGovern to recruit the campaign team to help him win the Democratic nomination in 1972—and that led him to our door to ask my mother for support.

18   Abandoning university was not part of the plan when we moved to the tiny village of Margaree Harbour on Cape Breton Island. I enrolled at St. Francis Xavier with all my friends from Margaree who were headed there in the fall. While registering

for classes, I found out I needed to pay $400. I phoned home. My father said we didn't have the money, so I took the bus back home over the Causeway. Waitressing and cooking in the summer months, collecting unemployment insurance in the winter so that my parents would have money for food, heat, and electricity, was my life for most of my twenties.

It was not a life completely divorced from politics. When the Progressive Conservative minority government of Joe Clark fell in 1979, I was profoundly disappointed by the negative advertising of the Pierre Trudeau Liberals. But by today's bleak standards, those ads were positively inspiring. Despairing of the lack of focus on issues, I thought we should have a way to inject environmental issues into a federal campaign that was devoid of them. Having phoned friends, activists, and colleagues in many provinces, I managed to convince eleven others in six provinces to take the plunge with me and run in high-profile ridings of powerful incumbents. It was clearly a *beau geste*. My friend Dr. Gordon Edwards of the Canadian Coalition for Nuclear Responsibility ran against Pierre Trudeau, and I ran against Trudeau's deputy prime minister, legendary parliamentarian Allan J. MacEachen. We knew we had no time to write a shared manifesto. And, in that time before the existence of the internet, developing a platform would be impractical in the time available. Then it hit me, and I phoned everyone to suggest that we be called "the small party" and that our foundational principles be based on E.F. Schumacher's wonderful book, *Small Is Beautiful: A Study of Economics as if People Mattered.*

When the 1980 campaign was over, I sold my car to pay my phone bill. Other early "small party" organizers continued to meet to discuss the benefits of starting a new political party. By 1983, the "small party" had become the Green Party. But that effort was led by others. My life had changed course once again. More accurately, I had gotten my life back on track toward what I had always wanted to do.

I got into law school without an undergraduate degree. On March 8, 1980, I was at a pub in Sydney, Cape Breton, for an International Women's Day event, having driven the two hours across the island with women friends to hear the wonderful feminist singer Rita MacNeil (not yet famous and a lot more radical than her public image later in her career). I ran into a woman lawyer who told me I should be in law school. When I explained that I had always wanted to practise law but that I didn't even have an undergrad degree, she opened the door to a whole new world of possibility.

Thanks to the women's movement, law schools had opened places for people who had been out of school and in the workforce. And I had an edge to get in. By then I had become known in Nova Scotia as an environmental campaigner. I had been part of an epic struggle, an amazing grassroots campaign that absorbed every ounce of my energy in the winter months over several years, opposing aerial insecticide spraying over Cape Breton's forests. Against all odds, we succeeded in protecting Cape Breton from pesticide spraying. I had to overcome a few hurdles to get into law school—writing the LSAT and submitting a letter of recommendation. Wracking my brain, I tried to think of someone suitable to write the required letter of reference, trying to think of anyone who had a legal background and also knew me well enough. I decided to ask Bill Clinton. I have no way of knowing what the admissions committee thought of receiving a letter from the governor of Arkansas about a waitress/cook/activist in Cape Breton. But because they had heard me debate pulp company executives in the media, and because the campaign to prevent aerial insecticide spraying had dominated the provincial news year after year, with our coalition against the spray winning every year, I became a candidate for law school.

I have so often been part of environmental campaigns against impossible odds. And so often, we have won. No campaign is ever won by one person. No campaign against impossible odds is ever

20

impossible. (See the excerpt from *The Phantom Tollbooth* at the end of this chapter. Words to live by.) Mobilizing large numbers of people to get off the couch and move to action is never the work of one person. So many people—volunteers, scientists, sometimes celebrities—are always part of winning campaigns. One of my friends described her networking as being a biodegradable crochet hook. I always think of the old proverb: "For want of a nail, the shoe was lost; for want of a shoe, the horse was lost; for want of the horse, the officer was lost; for want of the officer… " and so on until "the battle was lost."

In many campaigns, I have been blessed to be at the right place at the right time. I kept so many little nails in so many horseshoes. Without those nails, we could never have stopped pesticide spraying on Cape Breton's forests, or uranium mining in Nova Scotia, or the clear-cut logging of Lyell Island and the victory that is now Gwaii Haanas National Park Reserve. My dearest friends are those made in such campaigns. In stopping the logging of the southern third of Haida Gwaii, I made more than a friend of one of British Columbia's most extraordinary activists, Vicky Husband. We became something closer to sisters. Most of my books have been about winning these victories against all odds.

My first book, *Budworm Battles*, chronicles the years of grassroots activity in taking on an old, established giant multinational based in Sweden. Without intending to do more than stop the poisoning of my island, I ended up with a resumé to get back to school.

Being a law student at Dalhousie University was pure joy. I loved my new friends from all across Canada. And the bursaries from the Nova Scotia government allowed me more financial freedom than I had known for years. I can still remember the first time I was able to afford to go to a movie and the feeling of that movie ticket in my fingers as I stood in line at the Oxford Theatre.

More than anything else, I loved reading law. I loved sitting in a classroom listening to my professors. I loved arguing a legal

21

point. My most lasting lesson came from the late Graham Murray, who taught evidence. He punctuated his lectures by bringing his wooden cane down across his desk with a sharp "thwack!" and saying, "Develop the habit of thoroughness!"

Law school was interrupted by the most personally punishing of any environmental fight in my life—going to court to block the spraying of Agent Orange over those same Cape Breton forests by the same multinationals that had tried and failed to spray insecticides. One of the most amazing women I have ever known, June Callwood, wrote my mother saying, "This is a David and Goliath struggle, only, this time, Goliath has the slingshot."

The case occupied two years of our lives and cost my family the eighty acres of land my parents had first bought in Cape Breton with the plan of living there in retirement, overlooking the Bras d'Or Lakes. Whenever it felt as though the industry was grinding a boot into my neck, my brother, Geoffrey, would cheer me up with a slightly maniacal and exultant "We got the bastards on the run now!"

I missed my graduation from law school. I was cross-examining one of the industry's expert witnesses that day. Our lawyers were exhausted by the month-long trial, facing a battery of industry lawyers. Early that morning they realized that, with my graduation, if we filed the paperwork for me to be articled to one of them, the Nova Scotia procedural rules would allow me to conduct the cross-examination of the next witness.

I knew his research inside and out. It was our great good fortune that a U.S. Environmental Protection Agency researcher, whose examination of this witness had been pre-empted by Dow's out-of-court settlement with the U.S. government, sent us the witness's original field notes. The expert's published papers on the persistence of the herbicides and their depth in the soil were contradicted by the field notes. And the published papers appeared to falsify that information to minimize the risks of the chemicals. The witness was one of a stable of pro–Agent Orange experts

22

whom Dow used in many trials. It was critical to nail the cross-examination. One of the lawyers asked my mother to drive from Sydney, Cape Breton, to Halifax to file the papers before the witness could take the stand. The drive normally took five hours, but my mom made it in just over three hours. She called from Halifax, triumphant that she had set a new land speed record. It was no mystery why my father referred to driving with her as flying Air Stephanie. "Now that I'm here," she asked, "is there anything else you'd like me to do?"

"Sure," I said, "could you go to my graduation, say hi to my friends, and pick up my diploma?"

Despite heroic efforts, we lost the case. The judge ruled that Agent Orange was safe and had not caused any damage in Vietnam, nor had dioxin caused any serious problems in Seveso, Italy, where a factory explosion had led to the evacuation of the town. The decision was such a terrible blow that it rather took the fun out of practising law in Halifax.

The reality is that we prevented Cape Breton Island from being the last jurisdiction in North America to be sprayed with Agent Orange. By the time Judge Merlin Nunn ruled against our suit for a permanent injunction, the chemicals were no longer available in Canada. Dow and the U.S. government had reached a deal by which Dow Chemical voluntarily agreed to stop selling its old stock of 2,4,5-T to the few countries where Agent Orange had not been banned. That meant that, while 2,4,5-T remained legal in Canada, the forest industry could not find any for sale. The herbicides that had been purchased to be sprayed in Nova Scotia in the summer of 1982 were sprayed in New Brunswick instead.

But my actions cost my parents their beautiful property over the Bras d'Or Lakes. That was the hardest part. In tears, I told my father how deeply sorry I was. Without checking with him first, my mother had decided to sell the land.

Our lawyers were worried the industry would use the unpaid costs from the temporary injunction hearing to claim we were

23

"impecunious." The pulp company had set a deadline of the end of the week for us to pay. If we didn't, we were sure the company would then go to court claiming a large amount of money for "security for costs." If we couldn't pay, we would have lost our right to a trial to prevent the spraying of Agent Orange. My mom called a friend in Los Angeles, former Cape Bretoner and award-winning Hollywood director Daniel Petrie, and asked if he would buy our land. It was the only thing she could think of to find $15,000 within the week. He promised to send a cheque for what we owed the industry and to do the paperwork later for the sale of the land.

I thought my father would resent the fact that my mother and I had acted precipitously, losing our land, but he was so great. "If we have kept even one person from getting cancer from the spraying of Agent Orange, then it was worth it," he said.

We had always had a somewhat distant relationship, and I never loved him as much as at that moment.

We had weathered so many storms as a family—many of them because we were committed to being involved in the important struggles of our time. For my parents, it was a commitment to social change forged through the Depression, the Second World War, and then the Cold War and the arms race, the campaigns for nuclear disarmament, the civil rights movement, the rallies and protests to end the war in Vietnam. That they attached themselves so unflinchingly and generously to my crusades—even after their whims and romanticism led us to struggles of a different kind—losing our land when we were no longer wealthy was, while not surprising, deeply moving.

Since the day my mother placed that wooden angel over my crib, the world has changed in ways she could never have imagined. We think we understand time and history. Yet, our perceptions are always warped by the sense that the here and now is all there is. As I write this, I am as far removed from my grandfather's childhood, the stories of which I know by heart, as he was

24

from a time before the Civil War. The first Beatles hits are now as distant in time from this writing as the First World War was for my parents when I was born, but still it seems like yesterday.

Yet, how much has really changed? As Einstein said, we cannot change anything when we apply the rigid perceptions that created a problem to solving it. The climate crisis has replaced the mushroom cloud; denigrating environmentalists as threats to the national interest has replaced the red-baiting of the fifties; and regional conflict and loss of life in hot spot regions of the world have replaced the conflicts of Cold War proxies. So much represents progress, but overall, we are slipping backwards.

Since I was born, the world population has more than doubled—three billion to nearly seven billion. When Christ was born, there were two hundred million people on earth. It took fifteen hundred years for that number to double. And here we are, all seven billion of us, digging up the fossilized energy of the sun and releasing it so rapidly that we have actually changed the chemistry of the atmosphere.

I believe that we can emerge from the current set of interconnected threats healthier and stronger. I am, as Canadian global diplomat and environmentalist Maurice Strong used to say, "an operational optimist." We have no time for pessimists. We are out of time for procrastination. We really only have one way forward: to become active and save ourselves. And to do that, it helps to know who we are.

"Impossible" Is a Mutable Concept

SOME CONTEXT IF you have never read *The Phantom Tollbooth:* A little boy, Milo, bored and finding nothing to interest him, is suddenly thrust into a fantasy world when he drives his toy car through a mysterious gift of a toll booth. As his adventures progress, he is joined by a pompous bug and the Watchdog, who has a literal alarm clock in his side.

25

It falls to them to rescue the Princesses Rhyme and Reason from beyond the Mountains of Ignorance. They are dispatched by two kings, who are brothers in separate kingdoms: King Azaz the Unabridged, and the Mathemagician. This scene takes place as they are celebrated at their glorious return:

As the cheering continued, Rhyme leaned forward and touched Milo gently on the shoulder.

"They're cheering for you," she said with a smile.

"But I could never have done it," he objected, "without everyone else's help."

"That may be true," said Reason gravely, "but you had the courage to try; and what you can do is often simply a matter of what you will do."

"That's why," said Azaz, "there was one very important thing about your quest that we couldn't discuss until you returned."

"I remember," said Milo eagerly. "Tell me now."

"It was impossible," said the king, looking at the Mathemagician.

"Completely impossible," said the Mathemagician, looking at the king.

"Do you mean—" said the bug, who suddenly felt a bit faint.

"Yes, indeed," they repeated together; "but if we'd told you then, you might not have gone—and, as you've discovered, so many things are possible just as long as you don't know they're impossible."

And for the remainder of the ride Milo didn't utter a sound.

NORTON JUSTER, *The Phantom Tollbooth*[3]

Chapter Two

LEARNING THE WAYS
OF POWER AND POLITICS

THE PHONE LINE to Los Angeles lived up to the popular slogan of the day, "Long distance—the next best thing to being there," but my uncle Tom was not absorbing my news. "You're going to do what? You're going to become exactly what? Leave practising law to work for a right-wing, Conservative minister? Like a Jerry Falwell?"

It took a while to explain that by "minister" I meant minister of the environment and that by "conservative" I meant Progressive Conservative—a party that refused to oppose universal public access to medical care. That reassured him a bit.

It was certainly not an expected, nor an immediately desired, transition.

It was May 1986, and I had only relocated to the nation's capital the previous fall. The loss of the herbicide case had been so devastating that despite the kindness and support of the law firm that had hired me, I was no longer happy practising law in Halifax. Random encounters with the lawyers who had represented the industry and defended Agent Orange, and the occasional exchange with the judge who had ruled against us, would bring back the whole trauma of the case. Too many nights I would take the bus home, walking quickly to get back inside my apartment before breaking down in tears.

Looking for a change of scene, I applied to become the associate general counsel to the Public Interest Advocacy Centre in Ottawa. The job was a great opportunity to practise law, as the name suggests, in the public interest. I was, in fact, the only lawyer in the Ottawa office. My boss, legendary lawyer Andy Roman, was senior counsel and based in Toronto. I had a wonderful secretary, a certain freedom of action, and a great client list, anchored by the Consumers' Association of Canada and the National Anti-Poverty Organization (now known as Canada Without Poverty), and I was branching out to environmental groups like Friends of the Earth—a group I had helped found in 1978. In my spare time, I was co-chair, along with the splendid Tim Brodhead, of a major conference planned for Ottawa in June 1986—the third biennial Conference on the Fate of the Earth.

A law school classmate from Prince Edward Island phoned one day to ask if I could meet with his boss, another islander, Minister of the Environment Tom McMillan. Because the Conference on the Fate of the Earth was seeking government support for an international conference expecting to draw more than a thousand people, I was certain that was the reason for meeting, and I happily agreed.

Tom McMillan's agenda had nothing to do with funding our conference. Instead, he pitched me to join his political staff—known in government as "exempt staff," as in "exempt" from job security and from civil service rules, essentially "partisan staff." He explained that he wanted to deliver strong environmental policy, but that none of his political staff knew anything about the environment. "You can be my ambassador to the environmental movement and the environmental movement's ambassador to me." I wasn't convinced.

28   I called more than a few environmental movement friends for advice. The response was nearly unanimous: "What can it hurt? Go for it. You can always quit." The one exception was my old friend, dearly loved, Charles Caccia. I had first met Charles

when he was minister of the environment in the Cabinet of Pierre Trudeau. He met with me when we were in the midst of the court case opposing Agent Orange. Whereas bureaucrats from Health Canada testified that Agent Orange was safe and that the U.S. ban was politically motivated and based on "bad science," Charles Caccia was on our side. We had been friends ever since.

"Oh my god," he moaned in a deeply Italian, lugubrious voice. Charles Caccia was born in Milan and had studied forestry there. He was one of Canada's most consistent statesmen for the environment, but he was also a passionate Liberal. "Oh my god. These Conservatives are clever. They are diabolical. You must not do this. You will be only window dressing."

The next time I met with the boyishly good-looking minister of the environment, I explained that, although I liked him, I would not be a good choice for his staff. I think I even used Charles's words: "I could not be used for window dressing." I explained I was the kind of person who would quit on principle. He responded, "That is exactly why I want you to work in my office. Everyone knows you are the kind of person who would quit on principle."

I tried another tack. "You know I am not a Progressive Conservative?" Tom took it in stride, "I didn't think you were." As a shadow of concern crossed his face, he added, "But you are not anything else, are you?" I assured him of my essential nonpartisanship. "Great!" he said. Worries dispelled, he made the case again for how I should jump on board.

I could not think of a good reason to say no. As remote and hypothetical as it seemed at that moment, the possibility that I might be able to do some good was too important to pass up.

If I had known then what I know now about that offer, that job, and what it would be like to work in government, I would have said yes before he finished asking the question. 29

Sadly, in the end, I did resign on principle when federal environmental assessment law was violated in a political deal. In a complicated three-way trade, Saskatchewan premier Grant Devine received permits for the Rafferty-Alameda dams in exchange for concluding the negotiations for Grasslands National Park and for agreeing to translate the province's statutes into French. It was striking a blow for bilingualism that had been the PMO's primary objective. Despite my resignation, I never doubted that I had been extremely fortunate to have had the experience of being senior policy advisor. I learned how government works, when it is working. I learned how the Westminster parliamentary system works, when it is working, and we accomplished a huge amount. In the two years I worked as McMillan's senior policy advisor, we established five new national parks, including the miraculous negotiations for what is now Gwaii Haanas National Park Reserve on Haida Gwaii. We also negotiated the protocol to protect the ozone layer (known as the Montreal Protocol) and binding agreements with the seven eastern provinces to cut sulphur dioxide pollution in half, thus cutting acid rain in half, and then obtaining the same commitment from the U.S. government. We put in place the Canadian Environmental Protection Act and got permission to legislate the Canadian Environmental Assessment Act. The landmark work of the Brundtland Commission, the World Commission on Environment and Development (WCED), was fully supported by Prime Minister Brian Mulroney, and Canada helped to fund the work of the commission.

When Norwegian prime minister Gro Harlem Brundtland, chair of the WCED, brought the report to Ottawa, Mulroney met with her personally; in Washington, DC, no one in the White House was interested. Building on recommendations from the WCED report, *Our Common Future,* McMillan and Mulroney put in place the National Round Table on the Environment and the Economy. We had the benefit of superb advice from one of the planet's brain trusts on environmental policy, Jim MacNeill, the Canadian who had been secretary-general to the commission and who had been the primary author of the seminal report. He also had the intellectual and moral heritage of working in the early days of the Co-operative Commonwealth Federation (CCF) and serving as a deputy minister under Tommy Douglas when Douglas was Saskatchewan's premier.

On issue after issue, we brought forward policy designed to enhance our collective future. We listened to the Environment Canada scientists and Tom McMillan went to the cabinet table as the advocate for the environment. He didn't always walk away from the cabinet meetings with what he wanted, and we were often disappointed. (And as a non-Tory, I had a hard time with policies in other areas.) Nevertheless, the string of successes, especially in hindsight, was gobsmacking: the Great Lakes Water Quality Agreement, a treaty to save the ozone layer, a cleanup plan for the St. Lawrence River, bans on lead in gas and the herbicide alachlor, greater funding for environmental science, a national water policy, approval of the first cleanup plan for the toxic Sydney tar ponds, and more. The list is longer than what I can include here. The efforts to enhance environmental protections were not solely federal, as provincial ministers of the environment engaged in a healthy rivalry to outdo each other and Tom McMillan in a race for the top.

What is so striking now, nearly thirty years later, is that we were so much more advanced then. Parliament worked better. There was far more cross-party cooperation. And the Prime Minister's Office exerted almost no control over official statements and the actions of the department.

In conversations with other MPs, I often describe what it used to be like. One of my friends in the Conservative caucus was astonished when I described how little control the PMO had over our public statements and how often and effectively we cooperated across party lines. I told him how, in the past, parliamentary committees had been essentially non-partisan; they were places where—like gunslingers leaving their guns with the sheriff at the edge of town—you parked your partisanship at the door. You rolled up your sleeves and looked at the bill in question with only one thought: "Will this bill achieve its purpose? Can we make it better?"

I told my incredulous friend that the majority government of Brian Mulroney (one could even have called it, in the fashion of Harper's message management, a "strong, stable, conservative majority government," though we didn't at the time) allowed its MPs to accept or reject amendments from the opposition parties based on whether they were good ideas. One example is the Canadian Environmental Protection Act (CEPA) and its use of a priority substances list. At first reading, CEPA did not have a priority substances list. It was an opposition idea. Tom McMillan liked it, and the amendments from committee stayed in the bill.

These days, under Stephen Harper, Conservative MPs must ensure that bills pass unchanged from first reading to royal assent. No previous prime minister has established a nonsensical legislative process that rejects all amendments. Yet, Stephen Harper seems to believe that suggested improvements to legislation are partisan efforts to wound him—efforts that must be resisted even if they merely correct drafting errors. Since Harper achieved his majority, improvements proffered in the legislative process have been rejected more than 90 per cent of the time.[1] Even drafting errors remain, only to be corrected in subsequent bills.

My Conservative MP friend was astonished when I told him we never ran the minister's speeches past the Prime Minister's Office. Press releases, speeches, answers in Question Period—all were up to the minister to approve.

After my first year in his office, Tom asked me if I could write speeches. I think he asked me the first time because his speech writer was sick. I was never sure whether he liked my speeches better, or just appreciated the bargain of getting both a speech writer and a senior policy advisor, for the price of one, but after one speech, I became his speech writer.

We had a great system. He would half dictate and half emote

32

what he wanted to say in any given speech. I would take notes and then go off and write, squeezing drafting the speech in among all my other duties, sometimes pulling all-nighters. A few days later, we would collaborate in a creative editing process that often went on until he was walking to the podium. These days MPs find it almost impossible to believe. Like all ministers, the minister of environment was trusted to say what was on his mind. Nothing needed approval from the PMO. The same was true in the Martin and Chrétien administrations. It was obvious that approval from the prime minister was not needed by brilliant members of previous Liberal cabinets, like Stephen Owen and John Godfrey, who gave erudite and witty speeches without a note in front of them.

When I worked for Tom McMillan, there was also respect for the professionalism and competence of the federal civil service. Civil servants were not derided as "bureaucrats" or as useless ciphers. It was understood that the research and balance they brought to the table created better decisions. Prime Minister Mulroney paid attention to what his minister of the environment told him about science. It was in this atmosphere that I learned about climate change and the threat it posed.

We scoffed at the absurd politics and non-scientific nonsense south of the border. On acid rain, we had to contend with U.S. coal lobby propaganda that claimed Canada had invented the "fake" issue of acid rain in order to export Hydro-Québec's electricity. President Ronald Reagan even claimed that acid rain was caused by ducks. Nevertheless, Mulroney got President Reagan to agree to limit that pollution by 50 per cent.[2]

I had worked on the issue of acid rain before joining the minister's staff. I had gone to Washington, DC, with the Canadian Coalition on Acid Rain (funded, by the way, by Environment Canada to make sure that Congress got the message) to meet with congressmen and senators, walking the same marble corridors I had with my mom when she was delivering petitions about nuclear weapons testing.

I had also worked on the ozone layer, even in high school, protesting the chlorofluorocarbons (CFCs) in frivolous products like hairspray and deodorant, so it was a rare privilege to be part of the Montreal Protocol negotiations to save the ozone layer.

In 1987, when we were in the last stretch of the negotiations to control the release of ozone layer–destroying CFCs, the U.S. secretary of the interior, Don Hodel, suddenly noticed that the U.S. Environmental Protection Agency had been constructively participating. Hodel tried to derail negotiations, claiming that we should not threaten the excellent profits of DuPont. All we needed were broad-brimmed hats and some sunscreen.

The talks were deadlocked. Meeting at the Montreal headquarters for the International Civil Aviation Organization, the corridor chatter was more like a commercial transaction than a round of talks dedicated to saving life on earth. Competing economies with their own ozone-depleting producers vied for market share. We were in gridlock.

Tom McMillan sent me to check in with the key players. I ran from the hotel room of Lee Thomas, gracious South Carolinian, head of the U.S. Environmental Protection Agency, with messages for my boss. The European Union wasn't budging, and Thomas told me that the White House would give him no more room. As it was, U.S. Secretary of the Interior Don Hodel was trying to derail the treaty. Reagan wouldn't expand on the negotiating mandate Thomas had when he left Washington.

The core team of civil servants, negotiators, and scientists from Canada—Vic Buxton, Jon Allen, Steve Hart, Tim Leah, and others—worked round the clock. Within the EU, it was the Netherlands that raised objections on behalf of its industry. And the developing world argued that it was not fair to cancel its access to refrigeration (and the ozone-depleting Freons that provided it) when people were still dying from food spoilage.

And there was the crowd that said this was all bad science. That there might be something wrong with the ozone layer, but it was not due to these chemicals. Some of those who doubted CFCs were destroying the ozone layer were in the White House.

Canada pulled it off, though, in fairness, it was New Zealand's minister of the environment who found the compromise. The notion of "common but differentiated responsibilities"—that countries could be bound by the same treaty, but allowed different targets reflecting their domestic situation—was born in Montreal. The CEO of DuPont Canada, a company that had been making a killing in the chlorofluorocarbon business, was all smiles in endorsing the protocol. DuPont had developed a less ozone-depleting alternative.

The Montreal Protocol to protect the ozone layer has worked. Use of CFCs and other ozone depleters has been slashed. There are still too many loopholes, allowing the pesticide methyl bromide, for example. Methyl bromide, a pesticide primarily used in California's tomato and strawberry fields, is a triple threat: a toxic threat to the neighbouring environment, a carcinogenic threat to the workers, and, floating up to the stratosphere, a threat to the ozone layer. (Note for your fridge: do not buy California tomatoes or strawberries unless they are certified organic.) But, overall, damage to the ozone layer is being arrested, and there are even signs that the ozone layer is beginning to repair itself.

The Montreal Protocol was a complex agreement. It allowed developing countries to increase their use of CFCs by 15 per cent while industrialized countries had to reduce precipitously, by 50 per cent. All nations agreed to be governed by the science, accepting more aggressive action as understanding of the threat improved. And the protocol included access to trade sanctions to punish any country that ignored or violated the terms of the agreement.

Within the first few years of the agreement, the "parties" to the agreement (that is, those countries that have ratified a treaty) met in what are essentially legislatures of the agreement, called Conferences of the Parties, or COPs. Within the first few COPs, the science on ozone depletion was much stronger, and all nations, both industrialized and developing, had to move to virtual elimination of ozone-depleting substances.

Even as we were confronting the threats of acid rain and ozone depletion, Environment Canada scientists raised concerns about an even more serious threat. I learned about greenhouse gases and global warming sitting at the boardroom table on the 28th floor of Les Terrasses de la Chaudière, Environment Canada headquarters in Gatineau. As scientists briefed McMillan, I sat next to the chief of staff and absorbed the information. I was stunned by the scale of the threat.

It was a good time to learn climate science. It was before anyone had invented the idea that the science was controversial. It was before the "acid rain is caused by ducks" and "all we need is sunscreen to deal with the disappearing ozone layer" crowd got hold of the hundreds of millions of dollars it took to invent doubt about climate science.

That propaganda campaign found its feet in 1992 after the signing of the United Nations Framework Convention on Climate Change at the Rio Earth Summit. Jim MacNeill refers to the 1992 Earth Summit as the place where the "Carbon Club" was formed. I learned the science of climate change before the myth of doubt was invented.

Brian Mulroney did not doubt the climate science; neither did Margaret Thatcher. Back in the 1980s, scientists were warning us of what would happen if we did not limit greenhouse gas (GHG) emissions and protect forests. I can clearly remember the briefings. Scientists told us that, if we did not limit emissions from burning fossil fuels, the glaciers could start to retreat dramatically by 2030. They were wrong. The retreat began well before 2000. Scientists also told us that we could lose Arctic ice, and we are— only faster and sooner and more than we thought likely. Canada, the scientists explained, could have the same average rainfall, but the pattern would change. We could have long periods of drought

36

and then a major deluge with a month's worth of rain in a day. Warmer atmosphere contains more moisture than colder air, so global warming, the scientists told us, would bring more intense sudden downpours. And we would see more ice storms in southern Ontario and Quebec. There would be more evaporation on the Great Lakes, and water levels in the Great Lakes would fall. Oceans would expand because warmer water occupies more space than colder water, so sea levels would rise. And we learned that all these things would happen "unless we act to reduce greenhouse gases."

The last week of June 1988, Canada co-hosted the first major international conference on climate science. Both Norway's Prime Minister Gro Brundtland and Prime Minister Brian Mulroney were slated to open the conference, titled "Our Changing Atmosphere: Implications for Global Security." In anticipation of the climate conference, Environment Canada put out a series of news releases to try to bring the large, global, and somewhat abstract issue of climate change into a local focus. One release zeroed in on the threat to the ski industry from global warming and a loss of powder; another on the future challenges to prairie agriculture; another on the threat to shipments along the St. Lawrence as water levels drop and freighters get stranded; and another on the threat to Prince Edward Island because of the rise in sea level.

That last one gave rise to an emergency debate at Charlottetown city council. The news of a future rise in sea level shocked local councillors so much that they debated whether the issue was even much graver: Could the whole downtown redevelopment be put at risk? The front-page story in the Charlottetown *Guardian* (the paper with the motto "We cover the province like the dew") included a quote from local MP and Minister of Environment Tom McMillan to the effect that if we didn't act to stop the rise in sea level, our problems would be much bigger than the Charlottetown downtown redevelopment.

37

Oh, how we laughed. Tom's press secretary, Terry Collins, a former *Toronto Sun* reporter, said the whole thing reminded him of the imagined headline in the *Toronto Star* in the event of a nuclear war—"Nuclear holocaust snarls Metro traffic."

We laughed because we thought all our work would prevent these dreadful events from taking place at all. We laughed because in those heady days when governments listened to scientists and policy was largely formed around principles of responsible action in the public good, we thought averting the threat of global warming, while challenging, would be no more difficult than fighting acid rain and protecting the ozone layer.

We were wrong. We had not overestimated the acumen of our scientists whose modelling was accurate and only wrong to the extent that it underestimated the threat. We vastly underestimated the willingness of industry to mount monstrous campaigns aimed at buying time for fossil fuels before the inevitable shift to renewables and clean technology could take hold. A post-carbon economy must happen and will happen, but we have lost three decades and loaded the atmosphere year after year with billions of tonnes more greenhouse gases. And we will never get back the chances we had in the 1980s.

The 1988 Toronto climate conference itself was a great success. For me, it was a bittersweet triumph. Although I had worked hard to ensure its success, I had given the minister my terms: unless the Rafferty-Alameda dam deal was reversed, I would leave his office at the end of the conference.

Over four hundred scientists from all around the world participated in the Toronto climate conference. Then Canadian Ambassador to the United Nations Stephen Lewis chaired the meeting. One of Canada's most distinguished and conservative scientists, Dr. Kenneth Hare, went out on a limb and said climate change had already started, that the scorching heat wave seizing Toronto that week was beyond the parameters of "normal." Prime Minister Mulroney's opening address suggested that having completed the United Nations Convention on the Law of the Sea, we were now moving on to a Law of the Atmosphere. Action on acid rain and ozone depletion was the first plank in a global effort to protect our shared atmosphere. Action on climate change was next.

In a consensus statement that called on governments to reduce greenhouse gases globally by 20 per cent below 1988 levels by 2005, the scientists themselves had this to say:

> Humanity is conducting an unintended, uncontrolled, globally pervasive experiment whose ultimate consequences could be second only to global nuclear war.[3]

That was 1988, four years before the climate-denier public relations industry got its first nickel.

Nearly two decades later, when the documentary based on Al Gore's slide show became an unexpected hit, the denier industry, and many well-meaning people sucked in by a plausible series of common sense notions, asserted that somehow scientists were proposing a new theory that burning fossil fuels was responsible for observed changes in weather patterns. It was as if the self-aggrandizing claim "Al Gore invented the internet" was now being applied to climate science. But neither the claim that Al Gore invented climate science nor the common sense "skeptical claims" held water.

To the extent that the scientists in the mid-1980s were wrong, it was only that they underestimated the threat.

The science is pretty basic. I remember meeting with the *Globe and Mail* editorial board in the late 1990s. Terence Corcoran, climate denier and then a *Globe* columnist, was on the board. I love the way he writes, and I cracked up other board members, and even drew a smile from Terence, when I suggested it was a shame he didn't use his genius "for good instead of evil." Then the science editor at the *Globe and Mail*, Stephen Strauss, joined the argument on my side: "It's not complicated. Saying adding carbon dioxide to the atmosphere will lead to warming is like saying adding salt to water will lead to salt water."

Somehow, those straightforward explanations did not make it into the mainstream press. I never imagined that the clear understanding of climate science in the Mulroney administration would be subject to debate or dispute decades later.

As the June 1988 global climate conference came to a close, I left the minister's office. It almost felt like a graduation ceremony, saying goodbye to friends and to heroes like Stephen Lewis and Norwegian prime minister Gro Harlem Brundtland. It was not so much that I disagreed with the decision to grant the permits for dams in Saskatchewan without any environmental review as that I realized the betrayal meant that my job was gone. For the minister's chief of staff, a corporate executive on loan from Imperial Oil, to be capable of orchestrating such a cynical scheme meant I no longer had a role.

I had had two remarkable years in which all environmental policy making took place out in the open. I was consulted, and, with the minister's encouragement, so was the environmental movement. I had no interest in being a whistle-blower. I did not want the story to be about me. In the end, when my resignation was exposed by Barbara Robson, an award-winning journalist from the *Winnipeg Free Press*, the news coverage ended up being about me anyway. Suddenly the Manitoba legislature was in emergency debate about the deal, as the dams benefitted North Dakota but risked cutting off the water of the Souris River before it could loop back north and into Manitoba.

I was now unemployed, and my former boss, whom I had loved as a friend, denied that the dams had been approved in a political cal trade-off. Instead he told the media a variety of stories about what sort of bad person I was. The media spin ran the gamut from accusing me of blackmailing him for a huge severance package to claiming I was mentally unstable to alleging I made the whole thing up to ingratiate myself back into the environmental movement.

The timing was not good. News of my resignation broke within weeks of the writ for the fall 1993 election. On the night of the English-language leaders' debate, my mother was visiting me in Ottawa. Trying to stay awake through the debate, waiting and watching for any sign of an environmental question, I was shocked into wide-awake panic.

NDP leader Ed Broadbent lit into Brian Mulroney, saying the "environment minister's own advisor" quit over the failure to do environmental assessment of the dams in Saskatchewan. What caused me to sit bolt upright (thinking, "I'll never get a job in Ottawa again") was Mulroney's response: "I don't know why you would choose to take the word of Ms. May over the minister... " All I could think was "He knows my name." I was the only person not running for office attacked in the debates.

Before becoming unemployed, I had committed to an eco-tour vacation on a chartered boat in Gwaii Haanas. It was not an inexpensive vacation. It was a new venture involving a friend of mine who had campaigned to protect Gwaii Haanas from clear-cut logging. As a newly unemployed person, I regretted the impact on my depleted resources. The first week, I was a pampered tourist, but then the cook quit and I stayed the rest of the month, pitching in to cook for the newly arrived tourists. Whenever I could get out of the galley, I would go ashore to walk through the awe-inspiring forests with trees over one thousand years old. One day I borrowed a kayak and experienced the joy of navigating around the coastlines of deep green islands. I kayaked around Lyell Island, watching my paddle break the sun-dappled surface, casting droplets of waters in scattered prisms through the air. In that moment, I made a commitment to myself. I wrote it in my journal when I got to shore: "I don't want a job. I want a life!"

41

A Spiritual Message from an Economist

Let us return to the thought that life is a school. As one advances in school the tasks and examinations become more difficult. But the problems set by the Great Schoolmaster also become more meaningful and more to the point. Modern industry, by producing comfort on a scale unheard of in human history yet almost destroying the real educational function of daily work, quite clearly sets the most difficult examination task: how not to lose sight of the spiritual in the face of these overwhelming temptations...

Out of the tremendous examination set by this monstrous development many single individuals will emerge triumphant; uncorrupted and hence incorruptible. This is all that really matters.

This does not mean that we can wash our hands of this worldly failure; for only those can triumph who never cease for a moment, no matter what are the odds against them to fight evil and try to restore order. "Woe unto the world because of offenses! for it must needs be that offenses come; but woe to that man by whom offense cometh!" (Matthew 18:7). Anyone who merely "washes his hands" is one of those by whom offense comes.

E.F. SCHUMACHER, *Good Work* [4]

Chapter Three

WATCHING CANADA'S
GLOBAL REPUTATION
PLUMMET

AFTER MY WORK as senior policy advisor to the minister of environment ended, I was filled with a profound sadness and wanted nothing more than to head home to Cape Breton. But something held me in Ottawa. I realized I was the only environmentalist at the time who really knew how government worked. I decided to steady myself, to avoid jumping into a job, any job, out of panic. I had been able to practise law with the Public Interest Advocacy Centre by virtue of my Nova Scotia legal credentials and by keeping my work in federal court. I had deferred my Ontario call to the bar, but in the fall of 1988, nothing seemed as useful a life raft as signing up for the four-month bar admission course.

I was not certain if I wanted to practise law again, but I needed to do something productive, and structured, while I found my bearings. I supported myself with contract work and took the bar admission course.

Then one of my favourite friends, David Suzuki's wife, Tara Cullis, phoned to say that David had called from Brazil in tears. 43 The Amazon was in flames. To compound the many threats to the Amazon—mining, logging, burning—a new development threatened thousands of hectares of rainforest. An Amazonian indigenous leader, Paiakan of the Kaiapo, had asked for help to stop a dam on the Xingu River.

Tara asked whether I could help raise money to support the Kaiapo effort to stop the dam. I said yes. True, I had no job. I was not working for any organization. I was in the middle of the bar admission course while doing public policy research under contract to the Royal Society of Canada, but those were small objections. I asked one of my friends, NDP environment critic and Member of Parliament Jim Fulton, if I could use his phone and a desk to fundraise. Predictably, Jim turned a corner of his Parliament Hill office into my part-time Amazonian nerve centre.

With the extraordinary generosity of Gordon Lightfoot, who performed concerts in Toronto, Vancouver, and Ottawa, we raised $80,000 to help Paiakan organize a protest—an unprecedented mass gathering of indigenous peoples of the Amazon—to oppose the dam.

Over breakfast at Tara's hotel, the morning after the wildly successful event in Ottawa, with Gordon Lightfoot, David Suzuki, Margaret Atwood, and Paiakan, she told me she planned to go to Brazil to attend Paiakan's protest. She was worried that without western observers the indigenous people could be at risk. Rubber tapper and activist Chico Mendes's murder made both of us fear for Paiakan's safety. David was bound by contractual obligations and could not travel, so she asked me to come too. Checking the timing of the planned indigenous peoples' gathering in the northern Amazon, I realized it was just after my bar exams, so why not?

Our Canadian contingent was bound together by a commitment to protect the Amazonian rainforest and the Xingu River and to defend indigenous rights. Once David realized Tara was determined to go, he could not imagine staying behind. Contracts reorganized, he invited Gordon Lightfoot. Those who had volunteered to help raise the money realized that they too could buy a ticket and travel to the Amazon with Gordon Lightfoot and David

44

Suzuki. Tara and I found ourselves acting as impromptu travel agents for an increasingly large delegation. Sea Shepherd founder Paul Watson signed up, as did members of the team from the World Wildlife Fund, Friends of the Earth, Probe International, old friends from Environment Canada, scientists, and key leaders from First Nations. Representatives from the Cree, Nuu-chah-nulth, and Haida Nations all came in February 1989 to support the Kaiapo. The Canadian contingent was the largest group from outside Brazil, but we made less of a splash in the international media than the lone representative from the UK—a former British schoolteacher named Sting. The Amazonian protest succeeded in persuading the World Bank to reject funding for the dam.

In many ways, our Canadian contingent to the Amazon mirrored what Canada was then in the world. We were First Nations, arts, science, and activists. The Canadian embassy in Brasilia was helpful. Innovative diplomats there had found ways to help the emerging civil society movement within Brazil participate effectively in the Earth Summit.

Meanwhile, the adventure in Altamira, the site of the protest, introduced me to a Harvard University–based NGO dedicated to the survival of indigenous peoples around the world. Cultural Survival asked if I would be willing to establish a Canadian branch of the organization. It had only $24,000 in seed money but had incorporated in Canada and had a Canadian charitable number, so I decided to make that my next project. I used the funds to hire a smart organizer and then tried to find a way for me to support myself on other contracts. I never would have imagined that the part-time contract I took on to help cover Cultural Survival costs would become my life for the next seventeen years.

A volunteer called from the Ontario Sierra Club and asked me to set up a national presence for the Sierra Club of Canada. It was a classic NGO job offer: "We'd like to offer you a contract for $10,000 a year, but we haven't raised the money yet." With that, I became executive director of Sierra Club of Canada, opening the Ottawa office and running the organization from 1989 to 2006. Although most of my work was domestic, I was engaged in all the key global negotiations, notably the 1992 Earth Summit, the climate convention signed there, and the annual climate negotiations created by that treaty. Canada in the world always represented our nation in its many dimensions.

Traditionally, what has allowed Canada to make a difference in the world, as a relatively small player in the global economy and geopolitical power plays, is that we are not insular. We are, at least historically, internationalists. Until recently, we could be proud of the respect we had from the community of nations—respect that came, for example, when former prime minister Lester B. Pearson, then minister of external affairs, won the Nobel Peace Prize for resolving the 1956 Suez crisis and, in so doing, creating the UN Peacekeepers.

When a more recent minister of foreign affairs, Lloyd Axworthy, described Canada as "punching above our weight," we got it. His description of our role in the world as a "soft power" placed us in a position where we could do the most good. Those who studied geopolitical influence understood that such a strategy was the only way we could exert influence or maintain status on the world stage. The superpowers preferred a model in which they were hubs, having arranged other nations, whether allies or trading partners, on spokes, rigidly kept in orbit around them. In this way, the superpowers could maintain total dominance.

The only way Canada could have any influence was to be a trusted "honest broker." Our influence depended on being seen by developing countries and other industrialized nations as a bridge between North and South. As Paul Heinbecker, Canada's former ambassador to the United Nations, put it once to a Green Party forum on international affairs, the rest of the world judges Canada's importance in the world both by how well we get along with the United States and by how independently we chart our foreign policy from the White House.[1]

The strategy of making a difference by championing international engagement in human rights, peacekeeping, and environmental stewardship was not exclusively embraced by previous Liberal governments.

It was Progressive Conservative Brian Mulroney who took on the apartheid regime of South Africa. He defied an ideological ally in Margaret Thatcher when, in 1987, he led the charge for economic sanctions against South Africa from Commonwealth nations. Paul Heinbecker told me that, as sanctions appeared to be working, the Canadian business community asked Mulroney to lift them, claiming they had accomplished their goal. The former PM asked Heinbecker if he had any way to reach Nelson Mandela in jail and said he would only lift the sanctions if Nelson Mandela agreed. When Heinbecker managed to reach him, Mandela said it was not the time to lift sanctions. There is a reason that the first country Nelson Mandela visited after he was released from prison was Canada.

It was also under Brian Mulroney that key global treaties to protect the environment were negotiated. Attending the 1992 Rio Earth Summit, carrying my eleven-month-old daughter through the most child unfriendly workspace I had ever encountered, I could rely on many Canadian MPs to help me fold up the baby stroller. Our delegation included Liberal environment champion Charles Caccia and environment critic Paul Martin as well as friends from the NDP, like Jim Fulton, and a very youthful minister of the environment, Jean Charest. As a delegation, we were collegial and hard-working, and we worked across party lines for strong outcomes.

It would be a mistake to depict Mulroney as more or less "along for the ride." At Rio, Canada rescued the Convention on Biodiversity when the U.S., under George Bush (the elder), announced the U.S. would not sign the treaty. The fate of the biodiversity agreement hung in the balance as Japan and France appeared lukewarm to signing. Within twenty-four hours of Bush's backing off, Mulroney announced that Canada would sign and support the biodiversity pact. His decisive action staunched the threat of waning support. All major industrialized countries, other than the U.S., signed the treaty. Canada was the first country to both sign and ratify the conventions on biodiversity and climate change, ratifying before the end of 1992.

Canadians had a hand in drafting the UN Charter, the Law of the Sea, and the Universal Declaration of Human Rights, as well as establishing the International Criminal Court. In fact, when Heinbecker, as Canadian representative to the United Nations, was negotiating for Canada in the International Criminal Court deliberations in 2001, the Bush White House pressured Ottawa to have him fired. He wasn't.

The United Nations has been celebrated in Canada, far more than in the United States. But today there is a diminished level of trust in the UN, going back to former general and senator Roméo Dallaire's experience of the genocide in Rwanda, his courageous efforts to get the attention of powerful nations and the UN itself, and their contemptible failure to prevent the slaughter of innocents.

Still, other than the occasional delusional website, Canadians do not share the more extreme anti-UN views too often found in the U.S., with its fears of "black helicopters" and a demon "world government." Multilateralism is in our DNA. When the United Nations falls short, that failure is one worn by the community of nations. As Bill Clinton explained to a Nova Scotia audience at the Fox Harbour Golf Resort in 2007, we established the United Nations as a talk shop to find ways to talk our way back from the brink of nuclear war. To denounce it now as a "talk shop" is hardly reasonable. If we didn't have it, we would have to invent it.[2] In the room that summer evening, I saw a hundred business leaders nod in agreement. Even an inherently conservative Canadian crowd supports the fundamental preference for negotiation, consensus building, and peaceful solutions.

48

We understand as a people that when problems are global, we need global solutions.

Canada had been in the lead in applying global tools to address international environmental threats. The Montreal Protocol worked so well that it became the model for a new treaty to mandate reductions in greenhouse gases. By the time those negotiations wrapped up at COP3 of the Rio UN Framework Convention on Climate Change in Kyoto in 1997, all the key elements of the Montreal Protocol had been replicated to avert global warming—all, that is, except access to sanctions.

In 2001, when newly elected U.S. president George W. Bush tried to kill Kyoto, Canada, under Prime Minister Jean Chrétien, helped keep it alive. Chrétien dispatched his deputy prime minister, the late Herb Gray, to extended climate negotiations in The Hague, a special summer negotiation of COP6 talks. Gray's role was so pivotal that Sierra Club of Canada awarded him the organization's highest honour, the John Fraser Award for Environmental Achievement. Keeping Kyoto on track became a core element of our foreign policy.

Montreal played a key role once again when Canada hosted the COP11 climate talks in 2005. The negotiations at COP11 were particularly tricky. Because of the defection of the U.S. under Bush, Kyoto's entry into force (the point at which it became legally binding) had been incredibly delayed.

In 1997, the negotiators had accepted a double-barrelled ratification formula. For Kyoto to come into force, fifty-five countries needed to ratify, and those fifty-five countries had to represent at least 55 per cent of the greenhouse gas emissions in 1990. The U.S. represented 25 per cent of emissions in 1990, so Bush's refusal to ratify Kyoto meant it could not take legal effect until virtually every other industrialized country ratified. With over a hundred countries committed to Kyoto, it was not until February 2005, when Russia's ratification took effect, that the Kyoto Protocol entered into force.

At the Kyoto COP3 talks in 1997, it had been assumed entry into force would take place within a few years. The treaty set 2005 as the start of negotiations for Kyoto's second phase to be ready for when its first phase wound down in 2012. COP11 became the first meeting at which the parties to the Kyoto Protocol were to meet (first Meeting of Parties, so MOP1), a group including every country except the U.S., to plan for the next phase of Kyoto and keep up with Framework Convention on Climate Change work, where the U.S. was a voting party.

The Kyoto Protocol became legally binding, entering into force February 16, 2005.

With Canada committed to hosting the negotiations commencing November 28, 2005, Prime Minister Paul Martin faced an urgent deadline to present a viable plan to meet Kyoto. The previous Chrétien Liberal plans, one in 1995 and another in 2000, were jokes. They were voluntary and no one thought they would work. Although the pro-Kyoto coalition of municipalities, church groups, labour unions, and environmental groups celebrated the 2003 vote in the House of Commons that ratified the protocol, we were increasingly frustrated by the lack of a meaningful plan to reduce emissions domestically.

The 1993 Liberal platform, Chrétien's "Red Book," had pledged to meet the Toronto Conference target of reducing emissions by 20 per cent of 1988 levels by 2005. The Progressive Conservative 1993 election pledge, set by Mulroney's Cabinet in May 1990, was to hold greenhouse gas emissions at 1990 levels so that they would not increase by 2000. Compared with the Liberal Red Book pledge, the Progressive Conservative promise seemed weak. As emissions rose under the Liberals, Mulroney's target was looking increasingly good, as was his entire record.

50   Improving the Liberal climate record would take some doing. In the fall of 2004, Martin's PMO was trying to come up with a climate plan that would work. Just before Christmas, before the plan was sent to Cabinet for approval, the draft was sent to both

Environment Minister Stéphane Dion and Natural Resources Minister Herb Dhaliwal. No one would ever know quite how, but someone, the likely suspects being in the Department of Natural Resources, also sent the plan to Pierre Alvarez, head of the Canadian Association of Petroleum Producers. By January, cabinet members were reading about a plan they had not yet approved on the front page of the *Globe and Mail*. Bits of the draft plan, with negative critiques from Natural Resources Canada, were becoming a regular front-page feature.

Against a backdrop of internecine warfare in the Liberal Cabinet and cloak-and-dagger leaks to the press, the planned launch of the climate plan had to be shelved. It was supposed to be ready for the February 16 press conference at which Prime Minister Paul Martin would speak to the fact that on that day Kyoto entered into force. It was an ideal moment at which to announce a comprehensive and ambitious climate plan.

Instead, Martin was left with one "announce-able" climate measure at his February 16 press conference—Canada would host a round of climate negotiations in Montreal in the fall. Yawn, said the media. All you have to tell us is that more talks will happen? Environmental groups, desperate to see the draft plan implemented, ended up going to bat for Paul Martin to explain to an uninterested press corps that it was actually important for Canada to host the first-ever climate negotiation on North American soil. I had never before answered reporters' phone calls to defend a prime ministerial announcement.

The next deadline was to release the plan in time to set the stage for the budget. But the leaks to the press and the hand-to-hand combat within the bureaucracy and Cabinet to get any plan approved meant that there would be no national climate plan before the budget. In the event, Finance Minister Ralph Goodale brought out a budget with the $5 billion in climate spending needed for the plan, but without the overarching plan to explain how the spending fit into a Kyoto strategy.

It was April before the climate plan could be unveiled. Sté-phane Dion was finally able to explain the plan, which did not include a carbon tax but had a complex set of free-market measures to drive emission reductions. There was something meaningful in every category of climate action—help to get renewable energy projects and new clean tech to the market and measures to reduce waste in municipal infrastructure, improve the energy efficiencies of buildings, boost mass transit, and support new green jobs. The cornerstones were the market-based Large Final Emitters System, with the goal of a 45 megaton reduction and a cost of compliance capped at $15 per tonne (a disappointing concession), and a Climate Fund of $1 billion a year to purchase offsets and other climate reduction measures, with a priority on buying Canadian offsets from farmers, forestry, and other sectors with the potential to reduce emissions (with a goal of a reduction of up to 115 megatons a year).

The subsidies to the oil sands were still in there. The word around Ottawa was that the oil and gas industry was angry enough at seeing a climate plan. Taking away their subsidies would just make them more upset. As I pressed one senior official on this absurd inconsistency, he mischievously quipped, "But surely, you do not expect policy consistency from the government of Canada?"

The Pembina Institute reviewed the plan and concluded that although it would not get us to our Kyoto target (6 per cent below 1990 levels by 2012), it would get us within striking distance.

It was against all these domestic and international complexities that the curtain was set to rise on November 28, 2005, on the COP11–MOP1 negotiations in Montreal. Stéphane Dion had spent much of the previous year in shuttle diplomacy, building relations with the key ministers who would have to be swayed if the talks could meet their ambitious goals. When a country hosts a COP, its minister of environment does not represent the host country in the meetings. That minister, or sometimes a minister of foreign affairs, serves as the chair of the meeting and the president of the COP, with the mandate to move the whole room to agreement.

The agenda was daunting. COP11–MOP1 had to confirm all the operational rules for Kyoto while setting in place a timetable to negotiate Kyoto's next phase and navigating the objections of the Bush administration to the whole idea of legally mandated greenhouse gas reductions.

Environmental groups from around the world were in constant and close contact with news of how their governments could be expected to behave. As executive director of Sierra Club of Canada, I was charged with getting U.S. media, U.S. environmental groups, and U.S. celebrities to participate. Although all other post-Kyoto COPs had been ignored by the U.S. news media, we hoped our proximity to U.S. media would help raise Kyoto's profile there. I even asked Jon Stewart and *The Daily Show* to broadcast from Canada. I asked Al Gore to speak; he declined. I invited Bill Clinton and didn't get an answer. The assessment from the Climate Action Network, the key A-team of negotiation experts from the world's best climate action groups, was that the deck was stacked against Stéphane Dion. He had few allies going in, the Bush administration was spoiling for a fight, and there was not much room to manoeuvre.

And just when it seemed things couldn't get much worse, they did. The opposition parties (the Conservatives, NDP, and Bloc) threatened that they would bring forward a non-confidence vote on the opening day of the conference, defeat the minority Liberal government, and send Canadians to the polls unless Martin agreed to bring down his own government early in the new year. The opposition parties were spoiling for an election. Stephen Harper could see his main chance, and tragically the NDP and the Bloc were keener to see the Liberals defeated than to avoid putting Stephen Harper in 24 Sussex Drive.

It was almost impossible to believe. With so much riding on the climate negotiations, I couldn't believe that the NDP and the Bloc, parties that supported climate action, wouldn't wait at least a few weeks to bring down the Martin administration on a confidence motion that was already before Parliament. The media buzz was all about the ultimatum to Paul Martin. The number one topic in the media was whether Canadians would have an election that disrupted Christmas. No one was talking about the impact on the negotiations. Sierra Club of Canada put out a press release pointing out that "there is more at stake than Christmas."

Sure enough, November 28 dawned, and, as ten thousand people headed through the UN security screening at Palais des Congrès, the hotel workers in Montreal went out on strike, and then the government fell. Foreign dignitaries wondered if they had just landed in Zimbabwe. Stéphane Dion announced that until the close of the conference on December 9, he was no longer a Canadian politician. He worked for the UN and would devote all his attention to achieving a successful result at COP11.

Against all odds, he managed to pull it off. The Bush administration was more unhelpful than could have been imagined, but a masterful speech by Bill Clinton finessed their objections. Yes, at the last minute Clinton replied to my invitation, and I had the surreal experience of organizing private jets to get him to Montreal in time to speak on the very last day of the negotiations. As I scrambled to make it work, I knew either it would be all over by then or the speech might be helpful. It turned out to be a miracle.

The late Glen Davis, my friend and a philanthropist extraordinaire, laughed heartily when I phoned him from the crowded cubicle allotted to the Climate Action Network within the Palais des Congrès to ask if I could use his VISA card number to make a $10,000 deposit on a chartered jet. (He said yes.) I had not known that for security reasons former U.S. presidents are not allowed to fly commercial. I signed contracts, including clauses verifying de-icing meant extra costs. It was all done in a blur of little sleep and desperate efforts to shift the positions of the world's governments.

When the head of the U.S. delegation heard that the former president was scheduled to speak at a "side-event" sponsored by the City of Montreal, he was furious. "If Clinton gets in the building, we walk," is how the message was relayed to me. I told the Canadian negotiator who bore this grim news that, if things were that bad, I could un-invite him. "No," said one of our classiest negotiators, still in the foreign service and best left unnamed, "the government of Canada would never pressure an NGO to change plans. We will handle it."

Bill Clinton's address managed to so depoliticize the challenge that even the U.S. delegation knew it was beat. Clinton spoke for over an hour to a packed hall of more than five thousand international delegates. Without a note in front of him, he held them in the palm of his hand as he wove a narrative bridging his own observations of climate impacts with the threat to the world, the promise of a low-carbon economy, and the will to believe that together the world could respond before it is too late. We still went through another sleepless twenty-four hours, created by Russian objections, but by 7 AM on Saturday, December 9, 2005, we had the deal that no one thought was possible. We had saved climate action and breathed life into Kyoto.

Our joy was short-lived. A few months later our incoming prime minister sabotaged the agreement.

Public relations spin developed by Big Carbon started trumping science in the United States under George W. The same thing did not begin to happen in Canada until a public relations master manipulator arrived at 24 Sussex Drive.

Had Mr. Harper and his party not managed to form government, I would likely have continued in studies for a post–Sierra Club life as an Anglican priest. I had decided that I couldn't be executive director of Sierra Club forever and the organization needed renewal and new leadership. But I didn't want to go back to practising law; I wanted something different. My relationship with my church and God had always brought me comfort and joy, and I began studying theology, taking one class a semester at St. Paul's University in Ottawa. I imagined my future life as a parish priest. I wanted to learn Hebrew and Greek and read original texts. I had put politics out of my mind.

I remember telling my mother, as I checked off possible career options post–Sierra Club, "Well, I know I don't want to go back to a law firm, and I know I don't want to go into politics..."

As my mother's aunt Mary used to say, "Life has much more imagination than you or I."

By the spring of 2006, I was on a course to become the leader of the Green Party of Canada. I realized with dreadful clarity that when Canada works to undermine global progress on climate, we would "punch above our weight" there as well. And sure enough, ever since 2006, Canada's role in international fora has been to block progress toward reducing GHG globally.

Canadians will have heard of the climate "Fossil of the Day" award. Conservatives have gone so far as to claim that winning more Fossils of the Day than any other country—and thus repeatedly receiving the shameful distinction "Colossal Fossil"—is a "badge of honour."

What does not receive much media attention is the significance of the Fossil Awards. They are not measurements of a nation's domestic performance. Canada's fossils are not an international indictment of the oil sands or our failure to implement a comprehensive climate plan. The Fossil Awards are the product of a daily assessment by non-governmental observers during each year's COP climate talks and given to the country that has done the most to stall negotiations. "Fossil of the Day" is a measure of the country doing the most to block progress to save our collective future.

56   At every COP since Stephen Harper became Canada's prime minister, Canada has received the Colossal Fossil. That's quite the statement when one considers that, until 2008, his competition for Colossal Fossil was George W. Bush.

The UN General Assembly vote that gave "our" Security Council seat to Portugal should have been a wake-up call. Our international reputation not only is at risk, but is being savaged. We now have a government that not only is wilfully destroying decades of multilateral efforts, but also is putting Canada on the fringes. We are the only nation on earth to have legally withdrawn from the Kyoto Protocol, and we are no longer a significant part of UN peacekeeping missions.

But we are still punching above our weight. Only now we are using our diplomatic muscle to prevent agreement, to water down language, and to create the space for worse behaviour from others. Whereas in 1992 Mulroney shamed Japan and the UK into sticking with the Convention on Biodiversity, Harper has encouraged despicable behaviour in other countries. When as a newly installed prime minister, Stephen Harper renounced Kyoto targets in 2006, his decision to choose a weaker target, using 2006 as the base year, had the impact of weakening the entire treaty process. No other nation had dared to tamper with the negotiated agreement that 1990 was a commonly shared base year. There are many such examples. Canada is creating the space for weakened political will. Canada has become the worst country in the room.

At the 2011 COP17 in Durban, South Africa, Canada participated in the Kyoto discussions, weakening language to protect forests as sinks and pushing back on the idea of a second commitment period. If the EU wore the white hat, Canada was leading the black-hatted gang that robbed the payroll train.

As the Durban conference opened, a rumour was reported on the CTV *National News* that Canada planned not only to ignore the protocol but to legally withdraw. The news cast a pall on the negotiations.

In Ottawa, Environment Minister Peter Kent refused to confirm or deny the rumours. He did appear excruciatingly uncomfortable in his non-answers to reporters. "This is not the day," he said, when he would be able to confirm or deny.

The following week when he got to Durban, he met privately with the head of the UN agency that provides the secretariat to the Framework Convention on Climate Change, the brilliant Costa Rican diplomat Christiana Figueres. Relief spread through the corridors as word circulated that Kent had assured her Canada would not legally withdraw.

As the leader of the Green Party of Canada and an elected member of parliament, I was not allowed on the delegation of Canada. Although I was barred from attending the minister's briefings to the Canadian media in Durban (and I mean literally barred, as Environment Canada staff physically blocked the doors in case I tried to make a run at the closed doors), I made the daily trek to the off-site hotel where the briefings were held. As they left the briefing, reporters told me that Kent had denied telling Figueres that we were definitely going to stay in the protocol. As reported to me by several journalists, Kent had said, "I merely told her not to be concerned about any nasty surprises this week."

Later that day, I ran into Christiana Figueres. We were in our daily debrief of Green parliamentarians from around the world, and she wanted to speak with one of my colleagues in her capacity as environment minister for her country. I grabbed the chance to ask her what the Canadian environment minister had told her. Dressed impeccably in a pale yellow tailored suit, she was the epitome of elegance—cool and calm under pressure. She smiled and said, "We have nothing to worry about. He assured me Canada would not withdraw."

I was blunt. "That's not what he just told the Canadian media. He told them that he assured you only that there would be no nasty surprises this week." If I had punched her in the solar plexus, she couldn't have crumpled more. She literally slumped over. Her face fell. "No, no, that's not what he said to me."

All I could tell her was that as a Canadian parliamentarian, I was ashamed. Within hours of his return to Canada, Kent confirmed that Canada was sending the legally required one-year notification to withdraw from the Kyoto Protocol. He created the erroneous impression that there would be costs in penalties if we remained legally bound. Kent was actually very careful in his use of words to avoid claiming there were penalties. Tragically, the Kyoto Protocol was negotiated without any effective sanctions or penalties. There could be no "punishment" or cost to Canada to remain in the protocol in defiance of its terms.

One measure of how global regard for Canada has plummeted is in how Canadians are greeted by other delegates in international meetings. In 2006 and 2007 when Canada's about-face on trying to implement Kyoto was replaced with Harper's new policy to derail it, I would be asked by people from around the world, "What's happened to Canada?" Their faces would reflect concern, compassion. It was the same look of anguish and worry as if, running into an old friend at a high school reunion, we had just heard that an honours student from our year had been arrested for drug possession and child pornography. "What happened?"

By 2009, the attitude had shifted to one of impatience. "Don't tell us it's a minority. You people just re-elected that government. Why do you even bother to come here?"

By 2011 in Durban, as soon as people realized I was Canadian, they hated me. Unless they knew me from previous COPs, on first introduction, they assumed I was from Papua New Guinea. Breaking with decades of tradition, the Harper administration refuses to include opposition party MPs on the Canadian delegation. Previously, for decades, Canada went to world meetings as a country, with a range of views, not as representatives of a political party. At the Rio Earth Summit, as well as in every international negotiation of any importance, Mulroney's administration went well beyond including opposition parliamentarians. No more. There are no representatives from what is called "civil society" other than industry representatives, and no parliamentarians from the Opposition.

59

To be able to attend all key negotiations, I appealed to the head of a delegation I had always admired for strong, well-researched argument in COPs, Papua New Guinea. I offered my help in any role where they might need another pair of eyes and ears, note taker, and environmental legal analyst. I went to Durban with credentials from PNG. So, at first, on meeting someone new, they greeted me with a big smile, having looked at my badge and seen I was with Papua New Guinea. In 2013, at COP19, I was approached by the Afghanistan delegation to assist them in negotiations, so I had the same experience wearing the badge of a member of their delegation. As soon as I explained I was a Canadian MP, the torrent of anger would rush out. "Why do you people even bother to come to these talks? It would be better if you stayed away."

David Suzuki told me he had the same experience in Johannesburg at the Rio plus 20 conference in 2012. An African delegate got on an elevator with him and proceeded to tell him what the world thought of Canadians. David could no more redirect the anger by explaining who he was than I could by protesting, "But I am the leader of the Green Party. I don't agree with my country's positions in negotiations." I might as well have been claiming that I was an Avon Lady but didn't use Avon products. No sale.

As British journalist and noted climate author George Monbiot said in 2007, at the Toronto Green Living Show, "In the eyes of history, George Bush, John Howard, and Stephen Harper will be seen as more culpable than Neville Chamberlain."

In December 2005, when Canada hosted the last productive COP, when, against all odds, the conference delivered a positive result, I was proud of my country. The pride we felt was not in any one political party or any one person, though I continue to be grateful to Stéphane Dion for his unflinching courage. When the *New York Times* editorial celebrating success in Montreal praised the leadership of Canada and the UK in moving the world closer to meaningful action to save the climate, I was proud as a

Canadian. Yes, the world needed more Canada. What we were then. What we still have in us to be now.

Remarks by William J. Clinton

We just had a major television squib on our network news last week in America showing this new solar company out in California actually spraying nano-solar technology on thin sheets of aluminium, which may revolutionize the economics all over again. But, I want to make this one simple point. I hear people all the time when I say this—this is almost 2006—look at me in a slightly patronizing tone and say: "Oh, there he goes again. He's been saying this stuff for thirty years, and everybody knows this can only be a small part of the answer. Everybody knows solar and wind could never be anything as much as oil and coal and nuclear and all that. Everybody knows that." Well, that's just not true.

If you look at the geothermal capacity of Japan alone, they could produce over half their electricity with geothermal. If you look at wind, the difference in wind and solar, and traditional energy sources is that wind and solar are more like blackberries, cellphones, and flat-screen televisions—the more you use the cheaper it gets. Wind is going up to 30 per cent a year utilization— that means it doubles every two-and-a-half years. Every time it doubles, the price drops 20 per cent. If you want the price to drop faster, increase the capacity faster.

Last year, solar cell usage—had been going up 30 per cent per year—last year, it increased 57 per cent in one year. Every time the capacity doubles, the price drops 20 per cent. America spends roughly $180 billion (U.S.) a year on gasoline—varies depending on the price. If we spent half of that for seven years building windmills, then we generate more electricity from wind than any other source. It's just not true you can't take any of this to scale. It's just that we are sort of rooted in old patterns of organization and financing.

61

But, to make the main point, we know the capacity is there. In our country, 20 per cent of all electricity is consumed by lighting. If every home replaced every incandescent light bulb with a compact fluorescent one, which costs three times as much, lasts ten times as long, emits one-third as much greenhouse gases, every purchaser of a light bulb would save 25 to 40 per cent, no matter how many bulbs they purchased, just as long as they were being used. And we would cut the greenhouse gas emissions attributable to lighting in America by 50 per cent. We could create a lot of jobs transferring the production of light bulbs from incandescent to compact fluorescent—with another new technology just over the horizon I might add.

So, I just don't believe all of this stuff about how: "Well, all these things are nice to talk about, but we can't really get there." We're still wasting... most electric power plants waste 60 per cent of the base heat of the fuel going into them, whatever it is. You know, I saw Amory Lovins the other day at my Global Initiative—and a lot of you know him—but he's been out there saying this stuff for thirty years, and people have laughed at him for 90 per cent of his adult life. And no one's laughing anymore because we now know that conservation is good economics. Conservation creates energy just as much as alternative sources do.[3]

UNITED NATIONS CLIMATE CHANGE CONFERENCE (COP11/
COP/MOP1)
PALAIS DES CONGRÈS, MONTREAL, QUEBEC, CANADA, ON
DECEMBER 8, 2005

Chapter Four

RESISTING
ECONOMICS AS
RELIGION

W HEN I WAS a young woman, it slowly dawned on me that I was a feminist. As a teenager, I had not been drawn to the women's movement. My concerns were planetary and, day to day, I felt as capable as any man. When I was working in my family's business in my life in Cape Breton, I could carry a hundred-pound bag of flour up from storage, nail two-by-fours, and Sheetrock and plaster a perfect wall. It wasn't until I saw how much more the media trivialized and ridiculed me in environmental campaigns than it did the men that I began to recognize sexism. I tried to avoid hitting the issue head on by staying in the background and ensuring, whenever I could, that the older men in the group were the ones to do the media.

By the time I was practising law, my awareness of feminism took a new turn. I celebrated the accomplishments of the women's movement, knowing I had benefitted from programs initiated by the feminist wave, such as the one that allowed me to go to law school without an undergraduate degree. At the same time, I was critical of the women's movement's targets. True, we were taking our places in boardrooms and law firms. The 1950s model of women in the home had almost completely fallen away. Still, I couldn't help but wonder why we had not changed the male-dominated culture.

Patriarchy ruled. Models of exploitation and domination, of men over women, as well as of humans over nature, persisted. In reading thinkers like Rosemary Radford Ruether, an American feminist theologian, I began to see myself as an eco-feminist.

I came to believe we had made a mistake in segregating children from work life. Had we insisted that childcare be located in corporate offices and in pleasant spaces off the factory floor, in places that allowed parents greater contact with their small children on breaks throughout the workday, we might have undermined the corporate culture.

We were doing well in a patriarchal world. And sometimes we did that by trying to turn ourselves into what we thought men were. When I was still articling in the law firm, many of the secretaries were my friends. As my call to the bar approached, in a little chat in the coffee room, a secretary shocked me by saying she knew I wouldn't be her friend once I was a lawyer. The others agreed. "You all change," they said. And then they added that women lawyers made the worst bosses.

Women were taking our places in a corporate hierarchy defined by competition, exploitation, and patriarchy. The real world of women was still invisible to the economy. Women were the glue that held communities together by doing work that wasn't valued.

It was the feminist economists who began to figure this out. New Zealand economist Marilyn Waring, in *If Women Counted*, pointed out how the "real" economy discounts all the unpaid work of women that makes the world work.[1] And UK economist Hazel Henderson expressed the view that economics is a "form of brain damage" because it takes place disconnected from the natural world and remains rooted in models of patriarchy, hierarchy, and exploitation.[2]

64 As a feminist and a lawyer, I knew that one central way the women's movement measured our progress was by the gap in salaries. Equal work of equal value was not paid equally. Equal pay for work of equal value is a totally valid demand. The problem was

that it allowed a generation of women to equate self-worth with a certain level of salary. We were voluntarily commodifying our value to align with a market economy.

I recognized that, if I wanted to live a life in which my work aligned with my values, I would never earn as much as I could in a mainstream law firm. It was leaving my job in the minister's office that really made the line clear. I quit a $60,000 a year job and accepted setting up Cultural Survival Canada as a volunteer. To support myself in that decision, I was working for Sierra Club, as its first executive director, for $12,000 in the first year. And then for the next five years at $24,000 a year.

The most significant and life-altering event in my life occurred on July 17, 1991, when I ceased to exist primarily as the daughter of my mother and became the mother of my daughter. Nothing was as transformative as becoming a mother, not changes in nationality, financial position, or career. Nothing has brought more joy, and nothing matters enough to count as a feather's weight in comparison. And my precious daughter came in a package with half-siblings from her dad's previous marriages, giving me what I always wanted—a larger family than me on my own with one baby.

At Sierra Club I was on a contract, so I did not qualify for maternity leave. I went back to work when Victoria Cate was fourteen days' old and took her with me. For the next three years, we were never apart even one night. I used to imagine having a business card, like Paladin's in that old TV show *Have Gun—Will Travel*. Only mine would say "Have Baby—Will Travel."

In November 1991, Victoria Cate started teething in the middle of the World Women's Congress for a Healthy Planet in Miami, Florida. All things considered, a feminist gathering was a good place to be. As I looked at her and tried to figure out why my happy baby girl was suddenly screaming, a woman behind me in the auditorium said, "I am a pediatrician. She's teething. Go buy some oil of peppermint."

By that night, I had her happily in the baby sling while I danced barefoot in the sand with Bella Abzug, pioneering feminist and former congresswoman from Brooklyn. Bella had organized the conference under the umbrella of her group WEDO (Women's Environment and Development Organization). It was more than a bit surrealistic to be dancing with Bella Abzug as the real, live Leslie Gore belted out from the stage, "It's my party and I'll cry if I want to."

The economics of my life were amusing. Because I nursed my daughter, I avoided buying almost any baby paraphernalia. I used a cotton diaper service, and once she was eating, I made all her food from scratch with organic ingredients. Once, out of curiosity, I walked down the grocery aisle of baby stuff—a huge array of disposable diapers, wet naps, creams, plastic gizmos, and little bottles of baby food—and realized I wasn't buying any of it. I avoided wasting money and felt, somewhat subversively, that I was operating below the radar of the GDP.

After her dad and I separated when she was two, juggling my life as a single mother led me to many creative solutions as well as to frugal parenting. I confirmed the adage of my grandmother's era—waste not, want not. My household economy was an exercise in recycling and reuse, for the planet and to get through the month.

I fully embraced the Gandhian notion that "having more can never replace being more." This is a hard commitment to maintain when you are immersed in a consumer economy. I sought out those economists who rooted their theories (for that is all economics is, despite claims of science status) in support of a healthy community.

Today, economic growth is the unquestioned touchstone of every debate. The assumption that every issue—health care, criminal justice, the environment—must defer to the "real world" of the economy is so entrenched that it remains largely unexamined. What kind of economy improves society? What economic theories help meet human aspirations? Which ones are only about accumulating wealth for the few without regard for the many?

Economics is less a description of a discipline than a range of thought as broad as philosophy. Just as there are over two thousand denominations that call themselves Christian, there are a myriad of different strains and varieties of economists. There are Marxists, capitalists, and socialists, and within capitalists, there are Keynesians and the Chicago School, and those are just the big movements.

And the comparison to religious faith is apt. The economists associated with the Chicago School are as fervent and passionate about their theories as evangelicals are about their beliefs, and they do evangelize. Spreading out from Chicago like the original apostles, they have carried the gospel of small government, worship of the free market, deregulation, and liberalization of trade through reductions of tariff barriers far and wide.

Most of those whose theories still swirl in the world of economic debate were born at the beginning of the twentieth century, and one of the most influential, John Maynard Keynes, was born in 1883. John Kenneth Galbraith, E.F. Schumacher, and Milton Friedman were born within four years of each other.

The influences on them were, therefore, largely similar. Galbraith was born in rural Ontario, Friedman in Chicago, and Schumacher in Germany, though he moved to the UK to avoid Nazi rule. The contractions and tumult of the Great Depression and then the Second World War shaped all of their lives.

Schumacher's *Small Is Beautiful: A Study of Economics as if People Mattered* was the first book on economics that made a real impact on me; in homage to the book, as I've mentioned, we named our quixotic 1980 electoral effort "the small party." Schumacher's focus on what actually worked to support societies was brilliantly clear. "Production of local resources for local needs is the most rational way of economic life," he wrote.[3] His life story was extraordinary. While interned as an enemy alien and working as a farm labourer after he left Germany for the UK, he wrote a paper that caught the attention of John Maynard

Keynes, the most prominent economist of the era. Keynes managed to get Schumacher released from internment to start playing a role in government's economic planning.

Schumacher's writings ran headlong into the growing momentum of globalization, and his theories seemed to be a quaint anachronism.

It wasn't until I met James Tobin, Nobel Prize–winning economist, that I paid much attention to the events, particularly the Great Depression, that had influenced the competing economic theories of the best-known economists.

In 1999, on behalf of the Halifax Initiative, a coalition of non-governmental groups, I asked James Tobin to speak in Ottawa. We wanted him to explain his proposal for a global currency transaction tax, to be applied whenever one currency was traded for another. Support for the so-called Tobin Tax was growing, and NDP MP Bill Blaikie had introduced a motion in support of the Tobin Tax to the House of Commons. We worked hard to get it passed.

I was amazed Tobin agreed, as well as understandably nervous to be hosting one of the world's most respected economists. I needn't have been. He was down to earth, and his no-nonsense, non-intimidating explanation of his plan was "We have to cool down the hot money."

By "hot money" he was referring to the billions of dollars a day that changed hands, traded in the interest of making money on the small margins of difference between the value of the yen in the morning and the British pound the next day. Although some currency was traded for reasons of business or travel, huge, dislocating amounts of money traded hands in speculative transactions to enrich billionaires. It's fun while it lasts, but the amount of speculation had begun to threaten and undermine the stability of national currencies. Even the British pound had been devalued because of speculative trading by one billionaire, George Soros.

68

"We have to throw sand in the gears," said Tobin. He lamented that the International Monetary Fund no longer set currency rates, opening up the global casino in currency speculation. His proposal, a tiny 0.5 per cent tax on each transaction, would be too small to have an impact on legitimate transactions but would be large enough to discourage purely speculative transfers. The global currency tax would also create a pool of money to be used to fight poverty, promote education, and provide clean water.

It was what he said about the motivations of economists that stayed with me. Born in 1918, he was in the same demographic as Galbraith, Friedman, and Schumacher. He explained that people who had grown up during the Great Depression wanted to find a way to avoid another financial collapse that would have such a devastating effect on the mass of humanity. He and others chose to become economists to protect people from greed. Their goal was not to increase the wealth of the few, but to protect the masses of humanity from the recklessness of the most powerful and privileged.[4]

That was certainly the motivation of John Kenneth Galbraith. I knew Galbraith when I was a teenager helping my mother with fundraising events to support presidential candidates like Eugene McCarthy and George McGovern. It was in the living room of a wealthy host in Cheshire, Connecticut, that I heard John Kenneth Galbraith explain the threat to the U.S. posed by the military-industrial complex and the war in Vietnam. He placed his economic analysis at the service of humanity.

His classic 1954 bestseller on the causes of the Great Depression, *The Great Crash 1929*, has never been out of print. In it, the financial community itself stands condemned. "The sense of responsibility in the financial community for the community as a whole is not small. It is nearly nil."[5]

This could be said just as forcefully of the Wall Street masters of the universe who brought about the 2008 economic collapse. Having seen the Great Depression, Galbraith's generation of economists believed in the role of government and regulations to protect the majority, to create conditions for full employment, and to maintain healthy societies.

Somehow, Milton Friedman didn't get the memo. Like Galbraith, he played a role in the administration of Franklin Delano Roosevelt and the New Deal. Unlike most of those in his generation, Friedman rejected Keynes and his theories of the role of government in macroeconomic policy. Although Galbraith made sport of Friedman ("Milton Friedman's misfortune is that his economic policies have been tried"), it was Friedman and his Chicago School whose economic theories have become favoured by government since the late 1980s.

Reagonomics, Thatcher's economic prescription for the UK, and Mulroney's preference for trade liberalization—all followed a mantra made popular by Friedman. His theory elevated to nearly god-like status the miraculous wisdom of the free market. His theory prefers deregulation and industry self-regulation in its near fetishism for the private sector over public. It demonizes taxes and celebrates trade liberalization.

As in all propositions up for debate, there is a kernel of truth in each of these precepts. Clearly, big, bloated governments are not in the interest of a healthy economy or society. Cumbersome, inefficient regulations can impede economic well-being. I didn't survive years in a small business on the Cabot Trail without sharing my father's frustration at the absurd levels of paperwork foisted on us by every level of government. For the entertainment of tourists, as well as for his own amusement, my father maintained a bulletin board along the wall where bus tour passengers lined up to get to the restrooms. Under the banner headline, saying in red letters, "The Government of Canada never sleeps," he posted the most absurd of the recent memos and new regulations. It was a hit in the humour department.

The essence of the difference between the competing schools of economics was this: Does the economy exist to serve humanity, or vice versa? Is humanity merely one more resource to be consumed in the machine called the economy? Or are the economy and economic theory only useful insofar as they improve human

70

welfare? We are called back to the prescient subtitle of Schumacher's work: *A Study of Economics as if People Mattered.*

Those who seem to worship the economy embrace the Friedman religion. It appears to have come unglued from the reality that the economy and its theories are human constructs. Businesses exist to provide wealth and activity in support of society. Otherwise, the artificial beings called corporations would never have been allowed the fiction of legal personhood.

Globalization—operating under Friedman's prescriptions for trade liberalization, deregulation, privatization, and free markets—became the mania of the 1990s. As the decade dawned, the expectations had been profoundly different.

The 1990s were supposed to be the "turnaround decade." At the 1992 Earth Summit, there was a mood of optimism about the coming decade. There was the hope that we would start to wean ourselves of dependency on fossil fuel. We also hoped that with the collapse of the Soviet Union and the end of Communist rule over what had been the USSR, the West could ramp down its military spending. The turnaround decade was to be funded by the "peace dividend." The reduction in military spending would also allow the commitments in Rio to reduce global poverty to be met. Brian Mulroney recommitted Canada to the target identified by former prime minister Lester Pearson, when Pearson had served as chair of a global commission on poverty. The target, to devote 0.7 per cent of GDP to overseas development assistance, is no longer supported by Canada. The closest we ever came to reaching it, 0.45 per cent, occurred under Mulroney.

But the decade was usurped. Tragically, as the USSR broke apart, there was no Marshall Plan to help rebuild the Russian economy. Russia's Communist-controlled economy was quickly overtaken by organized crime. Public welfare in that country plummeted, as did life expectancy.

Meanwhile, the promised "Rio bargain" of increased development assistance coupled with transfer of green technologies

71

to the global South and a transition to reduced pollution in the industrialized North was abandoned. Aid was slashed. The Rio bargain was forgotten while pollution soared.

As Naomi Klein has commented, the climate movement ran into a terrible problem of "bad timing."[6] The climate talks moved on a parallel track with the neo-liberal agenda of global trade, deregulation, and privatization. The tracks were parallel, but the power invested was not.

The very same governments that had negotiated the Earth Summit treaties devoted more political will to the GATT Uruguay Round, which produced the World Trade Organization in 1995. The trade agreements had teeth, whereas the environmental treaties had a good set of gums.

At the same time that the WTO was created, the power of global corporations increased. In fact, the multinational corporations exerted more power than governments. This phenomenon became known as "corporate rule." As the relative power of the nation-state waned, the clout of the multinational corporation grew. Trade agreements aided the amassing of corporate power. Chapter 11 of NAFTA became the prototype for agreements referred to as "investor-state." In other words, these agreements were a direct commitment from governments (states) to protect foreign investors. For the first time in history, a foreign corporation was empowered to challenge and seek damages from governments whose decisions were perceived as reducing the corporation's expectation of profits. Democratically elected governments were voluntarily ceding their powers to private corporations.

The planet seemed to have become an "all you can eat" buffet for transnational corporations. Greenhouse gas levels were rising; forests were being razed; fish stocks were plummeting. As former senior economist to the World Bank Herman Daly commented, "We should not treat the planet as though it is a business in liquidation."[7]

One of the most cogent analyses of the excesses of the 1990s came from Ernst von Weizsäcker, German member of parliament and president of the Wuppertal Institute for Climate, Environment and Energy. Visiting Canada with a German parliamentary delegation studying NAFTA, he told Canadian parliamentarians that the rapacious assault on the planet's resources, just when we thought environmental policies were to be implemented, was due to the collapse of the Soviet Union. "As long as there was a threat of Communism, capitalism had to maintain a human face. It had to appear to be concerned with human welfare. But once Communism collapsed and the Cold War ended, capitalism began to have its head. Capitalism made the mistake of thinking it had won. In fact, Communism had collapsed under its own weight."[8]

In his own way, one of the world's wealthiest capitalists supported this view and further believed that capitalism's new triumphalism was a threat to capitalism itself. As billionaire George Soros testified to the U.S. Congress in September 1998, "To put it bluntly, the choice confronting us is whether we will regulate global financial markets internationally or leave it to each individual state to protect its interests as best it can. The latter course will surely lead to the breakdown of the gigantic circulatory system, which goes under the name of global capitalism."[9]

Soros was echoing another of the last century's great economists, J.A. Schumpeter. Schumpeter was an Austrian economist who served as that nation's finance minister as well as serving on faculties in Bonn and lecturing at Harvard. Schumpeter is remembered for many things, including inventing the concept of business cycles and identifying capitalism as an evolutionary process, through creative destruction. Reading trends, he asserted that capitalism would eventually destroy itself from within; that a brand of corporatism would become a threat to democracy, leading to a transition to social democracy.

Soros is likely the first billionaire to agree with him. When Soros was testifying to the U.S. Congress, the economy was teetering on the edge of disaster as a result of one dodgy speculative hedge fund. Long-Term Capital Management was one of those firms built by the smartest minds in trading, using mathematical models. With the skills of alchemists, they made billions from nothing. When things were good, it was easy money for investors, with a 40 per cent return on investment. No one asked if it was too good to be true. It was one of the first examples of casino capitalism (or at least, one of the first to land on the front pages). The firm was established in 1994 with the decision to deal in hedge funds to avoid the recent regulation of mutual funds. It was all money made from hedged bets.

And when things started tumbling down and this one small firm had amassed over $4 billion in debts, the decision was taken on Wall Street to bail it out. Failing that, Long-Term Capital Management threatened to take Wall Street down with it. Soros was nearly the only voice suggesting the need for regulation of speculative transactions.

Since then, we have seen the 2008 global crisis, in which "derivatives"—junk paper, highly leveraged mortgages, and other bad bets, traded as "financial products" by previously respectable companies like Lehman Brothers and Goldman Sachs—nearly destroyed the world's economy. Canada was largely spared because former finance minister Paul Martin had turned down demands from the large commercial banks to merge and go global. The Alliance Party at the time agreed with the banks and pressed for greater deregulation. It was Long-Term Capital Management all over again, but bigger.

The problem with greed is that, contrary to the rallying cry of Michael Douglas's character in the movie *Wall Street*, greed isn't good. It's not good for the planet, it's not good for the economy, and it's especially not good for a corporate entity steered by personal greed at the top. CEOs and their boards have a fiduciary duty to their shareholders. That duty is to provide dividends and prudent management of the corporation. That should be guided by a sense of responsibility to avoid risky behaviour. Addiction to strategies that only work in bubbles is risky because all bubbles inevitably burst.

Risky behaviour driven by personal greed brought down Enron. Risky behaviour fuelled by greed brought down Long-Term Capital Management. And although none of those responsible for the economic crisis of 2008 went to jail, no one could say their greedy, high-rolling, cocaine-fuelled risk taking was anything other than a disaster for the world.

The pain of that disaster was visited primarily on the people who could least afford it—people whose homes were foreclosed. Even though the White House shovelled billions to the banks, it forgot to require that the money go to help the people who needed help. The bankers just kept the money and gave themselves bonuses.

It was not always thus in the corporate world. My grandfather was a Wall Street maritime lawyer. Lawyers in his day eschewed those who skated too close to the edge of the letter of the law. "Sharp practice" it was called, and it was discouraged. "All I have is my good name" meant something. The era of "if you can get away with it, do it" was still decades away.

At first my father had loved his work at Aetna Life and Casualty. It was a big company but had the feeling of family when he first went to work there in the 1950s. By the time he quit to move to Cape Breton in 1972, he was assistant vice-president and treasurer, and he hated his job. In the 1950s, the company still cherished its values and history. Throughout the Depression, Aetna Life and Casualty had not laid off a single staff member. From the CEO to the janitor, everyone tightened belts, and the company continued to hold on to every single job and provide insurance coverage to its customers.

By the 1960s, a new CEO had been brought in with new values. Recruited by headhunters from outside the insurance industry, he demanded higher production, more efficiency, and layoffs. My father's efforts to keep his team intact failed as people who did not "produce" enough for the new CEO were fired.

Capitalism itself is not the problem. Human needs and the collective well-being of the country can be protected in any system. But capitalism must never be allowed to operate unfettered. Former governor of the Bank of Canada Mark Carney, now the British central banker, made the same point, "Just as any revolution eats its children, unchecked market fundamentalism can devour the social capital essential for the long-term dynamism of capitalism itself."[10]

A healthy economy requires government intervention. That's why we do not have child labour in Canada. That's why we insist on safe working conditions. Those are government interventions into the free market and no one questions them.

Measures taken at the end of the Great Depression had kept the financial system stable for over forty years, until the craze for deregulation nearly brought down whole economies. The 2008 crash may have started on Wall Street, but the contagion spread internationally. And while we still teeter with the aftershocks, no effective changes have been made to prevent speculative, non-productive high-risk trades from bringing it all down on our heads once again.

If the debate of the twentieth century was the relationship between the economy and humanity, the debate of the twenty-first century is the relationship between the economy and the planet.

It is a frequent observation that the words "economy" and "ecology" stem from the same root word, the Greek *oikos*. *Oikos* means home. Economy is the management of the home, and ecology is understanding its laws and systems. In that light, the two words are different sides of the same coin. That concept was moving into the heart of government policy with the creation of the National Round Table on the Environment and the Economy (NRTEE) in 1989. It grew out of the Brundtland Commission recommendations, accepted by former prime minister Brian Mulroney. In fact, I had worked on its creation when I was in Tom McMillan's office. The key concept was "sustainable development," a formula to align environmental and economic goals.

Our mantra was "If we change the way we make decisions, we'll change the kind of decisions we make." The original idea had been that the minister of finance would chair the high-powered group of leading CEOs and trade union and environmental group leaders. The very Canadian concept of consensus decision making in a multi-stakeholder process was taking off federally and provincially. Even the U.S. president created a commission on sustainability with high-powered corporate leaders. In the end, the NRTEE was not chaired by the minister of finance, but by a university president. David Johnston, then president of McGill University, went on to become Canada's Governor General.

I was appointed a member of the NRTEE in 1994, when Dr. Stuart Smith, former head of the Science Council, was serving as chair. As executive director of the Sierra Club of Canada, I took my place at the table with the head of the Canadian Chemical Producers Association, the CEO of Alcan, the owners of forest companies, and heads of the largest unions. Within a few years, Smith asked me to be vice-chair working with oilpatch executive Dee Parkinson-Marcoux, the other vice-chair. In 1998, in the months after the Kyoto climate conference, we ran a high-profile exercise: a citizens' jury on climate science in which all the "citizens" were Order of Canada recipients. Some were members of the Order of Canada by dint of selfless community volunteerism. Others, like Frank Augustyn, received their order for their contribution to Canadian culture. It was a practical application of the idea that environment and economy were two sides of the same coin.

We produced cutting-edge advice, even though, using Jim MacNeill's lovely turn of phrase, we were at "the cutting edge of the status quo." Still, compared with the deliberately ignorant policies

77

under Stephen Harper that have put economy and environment at opposite poles and considered them incompatible, the work was positively radical. We pulled together other multi-stakeholder groups to examine the ecological and economic catastrophe of the collapse of Atlantic Canada's cod fishery, charted a way to revitalize billions of dollars' worth of urban real estate labelled "brown fields," developed strategies for ecological tax reform, and assembled the case for the economic benefits of the transition away from fossil fuels. Some of our proposals resulted in immediate changes to government policy, resulting in, for example, increasing the donation of ecologically sensitive lands through reducing taxation on deemed capital gains.

The whole idea of a round table advising the prime minister to ensure that government policy was addressed—taking into account both ecology and economy and understanding that they were inevitably intertwined—seems a dream now. (By 2012, Stephen Harper repealed the act creating the NRTEE and disbanded it.) Still, the concepts are clear. There is no conflict between the environment and the economy.

Given free rein, however, the free-market approach undermines the relationship between natural systems and human wealth generation. Divorced from an appreciation that regulations and pricing signals are needed to correct for market failure, free market theory is an unmitigated disaster for human welfare and the planet. As Robert F. Kennedy Jr., environmental lawyer and great campaigner for the Natural Resources Defense Council, compellingly argues, pollution and waste are signs of market failure.

The free market deals with supply, demand, raw material, and labour. It can deal with elements of the economy with prices attached. Economics 101 makes it easy. Diagrams on the chalkboard cover these key concepts: as supply falters, the price goes up, and when a good is in oversupply, the price drops. All of these elements are in relationship and have values. The problem lies in

78

the so-called externalities. Everything without a monetary value falls off the chalkboard. Those things include the atmosphere, oceans, future generations, and other species.

José Lutzenberger was one of Brazil's best-known ecologists when he was made minister of environment in 1990. Formerly a chemist for transnational agri-business, he quit when he saw the impacts of intensive chemical agriculture. I had known him ever since he attended the 1988 Toronto climate conference, and he frequently visited Canada. Lutzenberger was a passionate critic of the market economy. He used to describe an imaginary scene where the *Mona Lisa* was put up for auction, but the only people in the room were children who begged in the street and shoe-shine boys. "The *Mona Lisa* would sell for fifty cents. The market does not establish the value of anything. It leaves out the interests of anyone without the money to spend. Future generations are not in the room."

Although Milton Friedman once famously said, "There is no free lunch," his theories and legacy treat the atmosphere as a free garbage dump, the oceans as a sewer, and future generations as unwitting creditors with no chance to collect on the capital they are owed. In other words, free-market fundamentalism gorges on free lunches wherever the system has failed to put down a marker through pricing or regulation.

In recent years, a whole new area of economic theory has blossomed in ecological economics. Gaylord Nelson, former U.S. senator and the creator of Earth Day, put the relationship between the economy and the environment best when he wrote, "The economy is a wholly owned subsidiary of the environment."[11]

The earth has limits. Global systems can and will disintegrate, reversing the processes of millennia that had created hospitable conditions for human success. It is not realistic to force the earth to meet economic theory. One is real; the other, a human construct. It is clearly past time to rethink economics to ensure we preserve global ecological conditions, allowing for human

79

survival, not to mention the survival of the other ten million or so species with which we share this uniquely hospitable rock in our solar system.

We could learn a lot about a healthy economy by modelling it on a healthy ecosystem. Healthy ecosystems are those that are diverse, with a large number of species. They are resilient, able to withstand the shocks of one predator or disease as a result of the multiplicity of food webs and systems. A simplified ecological system, such as thousands of hectares planted in one crop, is not resilient. It is incredibly vulnerable to insects, disease, or drought. Complex systems are inherently more stable.

The same is true of economies. Diversified economies provide more jobs while ensuring that a nasty shock to one part of the economy will not derail all of it. Regulation of the financial sector is essential, but so too is ensuring that small and medium-sized businesses are given optimum conditions in which to flourish. The economic equivalent of a healthy ecosystem is a series of robust supply chains, with value added to every raw material, strong local economic transactions, and competitiveness globally driven by innovation and new ideas.

A weak economic system is one predicated on large-volume exports of unfinished resources, a race to the bottom geared toward one product. In other words, the fixation on exports of bitumen and the distortion of our economy to put all our eggs in the bitumen basket is disastrous economic policy.

Similarly, an economic system predicated on unending growth is inherently unstable. It inevitably leads to boom-and-bust cycles. Smoothing out those cycles are the multiplicity of other industries and ancillary operations to each of the resources.

The mania for unending economic growth, particularly one predicated on increased consumption of energy and raw materials, is an insane position on a finite planet. The assumption that economic growth is a key indicator of economic health has only recently become attached to prevailing economic theory.

80

As Canadian economist Peter Victor pointed out in his excellent book, *Managing without Growth—Slower by Design, Not Disaster*, it was not until the 1950s that economic growth became an assumed goal of government policy. In fact, as Victor argues, it is more likely that a steady state economy can deliver a healthy economy and full employment, with minimal inequity between the richest and the poorest, than can an economic model demanding constant growth.[12]

The literature promoting a post-growth economic paradigm is growing nearly daily—Thomas Piketty's *Capital in the Twenty-First Century*, Tim Jackson's *Prosperity without Growth*, Gus Speth's *The Bridge at the End of the World: Capitalism, the Environment, and Crossing from Crisis to Sustainability*, David Korten's *Agenda for a New Economy: From Phantom Wealth to Real Wealth*, and Jeff Rubin's *The End of Growth*. It is simply not possible to ignore the work of serious economists who are noticing that the endless growth, speculative global casino economy is not working.

Canada has historically, and for a very long time, pursued a model of high-volume, low-value exports, whether in forests, fish, or bitumen. In writing my book on Canada's forests, I researched more than a century's worth of government-corporate relations in Canada. Over and over, I was amazed by the consistency with which generation after generation of political leaders, in province after province, would essentially say to any foreign corporation, "We have trees! We'll give them to you, and we won't charge taxes, but please open a mill and create jobs." Or, "We can guarantee you a supply of fish. Please build us a fish plant."

We were once hewers of wood and drawers of water. Now we are wasters of water and scrapers of bitumen. But now, we just say, "Take our resources." We no longer even demand the quid pro quo of "Build us an upgrader and refinery."

Where are the value-added jobs? Where is the diversification of an economy? The investment in new technologies? Clean tech? Innovations? Renewable energy?

Concentration of power, or oligarchy, is a threat to democracy. That's why we have antitrust laws and competition bureaus, not that we pay much attention to them anymore. But oligarchies are not a threat to politicians. They are helpful and friendly and quite efficient.

Another of Robert F. Kennedy Jr.'s observations about economics was the definitions of socialism, capitalism, and fascism. He explained that socialism is when the government controls the means of production.[13] Capitalism is when the private sector controls the means of production. And, according to Mussolini, fascism is when corporations control governments. As Mussolini put it, "Fascism should more appropriately be called Corporatism because it is a merger of state and corporate power."[14]

Flash back to Schumpeter: Is late-stage capitalism circling the drain as corporations rule over government policy?

A healthy democracy requires that the concentration of corporate power be reduced and that the multiplicity of private enterprise, big and small, be promoted. Encouraging innovation and entrepreneurship builds a healthier economy, one that looks more like an ecosystem. If we think like an ecosystem, wealth and jobs can increase, and use and waste of resources will be reduced. It is all quite doable, but not when those with power induce the whole of society to believe that curtailing greed, slowing the rapid exploitation of resources, and reducing corporate power are threats to prosperity. A healthy society and a prosperous economy can only be achieved when citizens demand that the economy exists to support society, not the other way around.

Economics as If Humanity Mattered

82   Too much and too long, we seem to have surrendered community excellence and community values in the mere accumulation of material things. Our gross national product... if we should judge America by that—counts air pollution and cigarette advertising,

and ambulances to clear our highways of carnage. It counts special locks for our doors and the jails for those who break them. It counts the destruction of our redwoods and the loss of our natural wonder in chaotic sprawl. It counts napalm and the cost of a nuclear warhead, and armored cars for police who fight riots in our streets. It counts Whitman's rifle and Speck's knife, and the television programs which glorify violence in order to sell toys to our children.

Yet the gross national product does not allow for the health of our children, the quality of their education, or the joy of their play. It does not include the beauty of our poetry or the strength of our marriages; the intelligence of our public debate or the integrity of our public officials. It measures neither our wit nor our courage; neither our wisdom nor our learning; neither our compassion nor our devotion to our country; it measures everything, in short, except that which makes life worthwhile. And it tells us everything about America except why we are proud that we are Americans.

ROBERT F. KENNEDY, FROM A SPEECH HE GAVE IN 1968,
JUST WEEKS BEFORE HIS ASSASSINATION[15]

For all their power and vitality, markets are only tools. They make a good servant but a bad master and a worse religion. They can be used to accomplish many important tasks, but they can't do everything, and it's a dangerous delusion to begin to believe that they can, especially when they threaten to replace ethics or politics. America may now be discovering this, and has begun its retreat from the recent flirtation with economic fundamentalism. That theology treats living things as dead, nature as a nuisance, several billion years' design experience as casually discardable, and the future as worthless.

83

PAUL HAWKEN, AMORY LOVINS, AND L. HUNTER LOVINS,
Natural Capitalism[16]

Humans are complex creatures. We have a demonstrated capacity for hatred, violence, competition, and greed. We have as well a demonstrated capacity for love, tenderness, co-operation, and compassion. Healthy societies nurture the latter and in so doing create an abundance of those things that are most important to the quality of our living. Dysfunctional societies nurture the former and in so doing create scarcity and deprivation. A healthy society makes it easy to live in balance with the environment, whereas a dysfunctional society makes it nearly impossible. Whether we organize our societies for social and environmental health or for dysfunction is a choice that is ours to make.

DAVID KORTEN, ECONOMIST AND INTERNATIONALIST[17]

The modern conservative is engaged in one of man's oldest exercises in moral philosophy; that is, the search for a superior moral justification for selfishness.

JOHN KENNETH GALBRAITH[18]

Chapter Five

BECOMING LEADER
OF THE GREEN PARTY

IT HAD TO be the most embarrassing credit interview ever—embarrassing both for me and for the woman from the Ottawa Women's Credit Union who had to ask the questions.

"All right, you'd like a $10,000 line of credit. Let's start with revenue. How much do you earn?"

"Well, actually... I am unemployed. I just quit my job."

"I see. How about assets? Do you own your car? How much are your payments?"

With a sinking feeling about the whole proposition, I got the words out. "I don't have a car."

She remained remarkably chipper, though I did see a crease forming on her forehead, "Okay, do you own your home?"

"Well, it's really my ex-husband's house and we have a mortgage."

Then the question I had not seen coming: "What do you want the line of credit *for*? Home renovations?"

I swallowed hard and answered in a contrite whisper, "I need it to run for the leadership of a federal political party." I didn't think telling her it was the Green Party would help.

I had come to the conclusion that everything I had worked for over the last three decades and everything I cared about was at risk of being dismantled by our newly installed prime minister.

Becoming leader of the Green Party was my best option for changing Canadian politics. But to run for the leadership, I had to become a member of the Green Party. As executive director of Sierra Club of Canada, however, I could not be partisan. Joining a political party was a no-no. So I had to quit my job to become a member. And luckily, the Women's Credit Union gave me the loan I needed to vie for the leadership.

In 2006, Stephen Harper had enjoyed only a minority government. There could be an election at any time. Given the prevailing political dynamic, I didn't see any hope of a different electoral result.

In 2005, when Paul Martin had a minority Liberal government, the NDP and the Conservatives began working together to destroy the Liberal Party. The long-term plan was not just to topple one Liberal prime minister but to permanently destroy the Liberal Party. Although political watchers knew this to be true, the rank and file New Democrat did not. It seemed impossible that their party would collaborate with the Conservatives.

Although they were polar opposites on the political spectrum, the Conservatives and the NDP, with support from the Bloc, brought down the minority Liberal government of Paul Martin in November 2005, triggering an election campaign. Throughout that 2005–6 campaign, the NDP avoided attacking Harper and kept up a steady stream of television ads focussing on the Liberal sponsorship scandal. The NDP also avoided, as much as possible, mention of climate or Kyoto.

It was the rational, politically smart thing to do. Talking about climate and Stephen Harper's opposition to Kyoto would risk driving soft NDP support to the Liberals. It was clear to NDP strategists that that is what had happened in the dying days of the 2004 election campaign. Liberal leader Paul Martin had crisscrossed the country saying that the NDP and Liberal values came from the "same wellspring," that Harper was the threat, and that the best way to stop him was to vote Liberal.

In 2004, the NDP had warned voters about Stephen Harper and his policies. Inadvertently, the NDP messages had echoed the Liberal message, and enough NDP voters migrated to the Liberals to keep them in power. It must have been galling to the NDP strategists in their post-election debriefs. They must have vowed not to allow it to happen again.

The NDP and the Conservatives bonded around one concept: the enemy of my enemy is my friend. Thus, the strangest bedfellows in Canadian history snuggled up, proving the aphorism that politics makes strange bedfellows indeed.

The toxin in our electoral system is that, unlike virtually all other modern democracies, Canada has a voting system that discounts all the votes from each district for anyone other than the winning candidate—riding by riding. This system, invented when people thought the Earth was flat, is called first past the post. Among modern industrialized countries, only the U.S., the UK, and Canada still run elections this way. Even though the majority of voters clearly did not want Stephen Harper and his party to form government, all it took was a minority in riding after riding to vote Conservative in 2006 for Stephen Harper to form a minority government. With partisanship trumping common sense, it seemed the NDP would continue to help increase the number of Conservative seats, even if the Conservative vote remained stagnant. Meanwhile, the Liberals would attack the NDP and ignore rare openings for cooperation.

The predictable and dismal dynamic of federal politics needed to change. Things needed to be shaken up. The best idea I could come up with was to become the leader of the Green Party. Clearly, if that was my best idea, there were not a lot of good ones from which to choose.

If I were concerned about vote splitting between the Liberals and the NDP, it might seem counterintuitive that my solution was to devote my energies to electing Green MPs. But I was not concerned about "vote splitting," a term I loathe. Votes don't split and

87

parties don't "own" a vote. A party has no predetermined right to the votes it earned in the previous election. Voting blocks are not chess pieces to be moved around on a board. Democracy is not a game.

My concern was that, because of the perverse impacts of first past the post, no party would ever admit another party had a good idea. Rather, to hold onto its vote, a party would launch blistering salvos at another party with policies potentially more acceptable to its own base. The first past the post voting system creates the intensity of hyper-partisan venom in Canadian politics. It is the parties that have the most in common that will attack each other most viciously.

It is only because of the first past the post voting system that progressive voters are lured to the demon "strategic voting." NDP or Green voters might hold their noses and vote Liberal, thinking their vote could block a Conservative win, though sometimes they guess wrong and help the Conservatives. Voting out of fear simply cannot be a good idea.

Something was needed to change the dynamic. Somehow I convinced myself that a political leader who told the truth all the time, even if it meant defending people in other political parties, might just be the wild card that restored public faith in Canadian politics. Reading over the Green Party policies, I was pleased to find a solid foundation in issues of social justice and international policies, in addition to the expected environmental planks. Running for leader of the Green Party began to take shape in my mind as a way to reawaken interest in politics among the disillusioned.

The most alarming development was the number of Canadians who simply did not vote at all. Turned off by politics, they were dropping out. Could a different approach empower them to claim their power and get back to voting? But in a crowded field of parties, where lying about others was common to gain a short-term advantage, why would people believe me? After all, I was becoming a politician. If media covered what I said (and it would be harder to get media coverage as leader of the Green Party than as executive director of Sierra Club), I might be able to help citizens engage and vote for what they really wanted—to vote from hope and conviction, not from fear.

Winning the leadership was not a foregone conclusion. A vigorous leadership race followed, and I thought, "If I don't win, I will have dodged that bullet and can do something less hard."

I wasn't sure it would work, but I was sure of two things: Stephen Harper was not open to persuasion to act on climate change or environmental causes in general, and working from the helm of an environmental group would be ineffective in the new political reality.

The reason for the latter was that the Canada Revenue Agency (CRA) rules were morphing. As a result of complaints first from Reform and then from Alliance and Conservative MPs, the CRA, for the first time ever, in the 2006 election sent warning letters to charities across Canada. Whether these charities protected women from violence, provided development assistance overseas, or advocated for the physically challenged or the environment, all charities were told to be silent during the election campaign or risk losing their charitable status. Organizations working in the public interest could no longer speak clearly about issues during election campaigns.

It had always been clear that charities could not wade into partisan politics. Certainly it would be wrong for a non-government group to run an ad endorsing a political party and expect to retain charitable status.

However, before the 2006 election, it was routine for charities to send questionnaires to political parties and publish the responses. It was not a partisan activity; it was public education. But lawyers from the larger environmental organizations reading the new CRA circular became convinced that even publishing a survey, with no editorial comment, might violate the CRA rules and jeopardize a group's charitable status.

That translated into less information just when voters needed *more* to know who was dissembling and who was telling the truth.

The second thing about which I was very sure was that Stephen Harper, unlike any previous prime minister, would not accept the imperative for climate action. Had I believed he was open to persuasion, I would have stayed with Sierra Club. Through my work in Ottawa, as well as occasional overlaps in our children's school activities, I had known Stephen Harper for years. Ever since he had become leader of the Alliance Party, I had tried to reach him directly, relying on a number of Alliance MPs with whom I worked on issues where Sierra Club policies aligned with theirs, primarily opposition to nuclear power. Stephen Harper and I had met often, but briefly. Once, when MP Monte Solberg had managed to organize a meeting for a number of environmental groups with the Alliance caucus, Harper bolted for the door within the first five minutes.

One of his environment critics, a Conservative MP, told me that "Stephen will never accept Kyoto. He'll always see it as one of those UN things."

Before turning my life upside down, resigning from Sierra Club, becoming unemployed, and making a perilous bid to become leader of the Green Party, I thought it was worth one last attempt to reach the new prime minister.

In spring 2006 I talked to my old Tory contacts from my time in McMillan's office and told them we needed to deliver a clear message to the new prime minister that protecting the environment and acting on the climate crisis were not partisan issues. The best advice I received for how to deliver that message led to a rather elaborate stratagem that involved reorganizing and repeating the "Greenest Prime Minister" celebration of the previous year.

90   In 2005, *Corporate Knights* magazine had convened a jury of environmental activists, academics, and experts and asked us to vote on which of Canada's prime ministers deserved to be designated "Greenest PM." Nominations went back to Sir John A.

Macdonald, and the winner was Brian Mulroney. The award for Canada's Greenest Prime Minister had been presented to Brian Mulroney on World Environment Day, June 5, 2005. But the former prime minister had been gravely ill, in hospital, and Barbara McDougall, his minister for foreign affairs, accepted the award in his stead.

One of my contacts from the Mulroney era, a long-standing Conservative, suggested: "You know, the boss really loved that he got that award and really regretted missing the ceremony. Why not have a big event in Ottawa and present that award again? Invite Harper and let him see how much Mulroney accomplished and that Conservatives can get credit for environmental accomplishments."

I called *Corporate Knights* editor Toby Heaps and asked him if the magazine would consider such an event. He immediately booked the Chateau Laurier ballroom for Earth Day 2006. It turned out to be the hottest ticket in town. Unbeknownst to us as we set the wheels in motion, it was the first time former prime minister Mulroney had given a speech in Ottawa since he had left office. Every Conservative wanted to be in the room, and a lot of non-Conservatives did too. I was asked to represent the jury in summarizing Mulroney's achievements, Ben Mulroney was the MC, and Rick Mercer was part of the program.

I was seated at the head table, wedged tightly between Quebec premier Jean Charest, who had been a friend since he was a very young environment minister at the Rio Earth Summit, and the new prime minister, Stephen Harper. Mila Mulroney was seated next to Stephen Harper, with Brian Mulroney and Sheila Copps across from us. My old boss Tom McMillan was there—the first time we had seen each other in eighteen years. It was a rare evening of political goodwill and high spirits.

I had seen a draft of Mulroney's speech and knew he was going to deliver a strong endorsement of climate action, invoking the scientific consensus from the 1988 conference, touching on the

91

successful effort to reduce acid rain, and calling for the reduction of greenhouse gases in ways that would not damage our economy.

Stephen Harper had accepted the invitation to attend and to introduce Brian Mulroney. I had reached out to people close to Harper to suggest some easy and low-cost green announcements he could make from the podium. It would be a great way for the new prime minister to test the green waters, in a room full of wildly enthusiastic Conservatives.

My hopes that Stephen Harper would jettison his hostility to environmental goals were dashed as I listened to his introduction. He lauded Brian Mulroney for winning back-to-back Conservative majorities. He praised him to the skies for his business acumen before entering politics. It was almost impossible to believe that at a dinner on Earth Day to celebrate the environmental accomplishments of the former prime minister and honour him as the "Greenest Prime Minister," Stephen Harper was incapable of saying anything related to the event. The words "environment," "ecology," "climate," "acid rain," "earth," and "green" never passed his lips. It was like a sportscaster ignoring the game to broadcast the stock market returns. It was stunning.

My days as a non-partisan environmental lawyer and activist were over. I had to jump into the partisan world of politics with both feet or watch from the sidelines as the first prime minister in history to actively loathe the environmental movement and all it cared about reversed our halting, limited environmental progress.

The way change had happened in the past and the ability to influence governments of various stripes were gone. Protecting the environment through the steady and time-worn methods of building a case, launching a campaign, getting public support, and persuading people in power to change bad plans into good ones had become a Monty Python sketch. It was a Dead Parrot.

All previous governments I had ever tried to influence—whether Progressive Conservative or Liberal federal governments or provincial New Democratic Party or Socred administrations—had responded to public pressure. All previous political administrations had cared about public opinion.

When Tom McMillan told Brian Mulroney that we were getting more letters about saving South Moresby (now Gwaii Haanas) than we were getting about acid rain, Mulroney became interested in saving South Moresby. When polling in the late 1980s showed that the majority of Canadians, at levels of 80 per cent and more, placed the environment among their top concerns, the Mulroney administration put more money into Environment Canada, elevated the importance of the department, and passed new laws to protect the natural world.

But this was a Brave New World of manipulative political management. It was clear Stephen Harper would never be influenced by public opinion. His approach to politics was different. If the public didn't want what he was selling, he'd simply tailor his message, target its delivery, and get just enough voters to vote for his brand of conservatism to win seats. He would never overtly campaign to kill environmental laws or worsen the climate crisis. His machine was too astute to ignore the views of most Canadians. He never mentioned Kyoto in the 2005–6 campaign and certainly never made a campaign pledge to cancel all climate programs and reject Kyoto targets as legally binding on Canada. Yet that is exactly what he did within weeks of becoming prime minister. No vote was needed in the House of Commons for the new prime minister, with a fragile, minority government, to reverse the work of decades.

Similarly, the Conservative platform never mentioned a desire to kill the Law Reform Commission, eliminate the position of ambassador to the circumpolar north, cancel programs in First Nations communities to combat cigarette addiction, or eliminate the position of science advisor to the prime minister. Yet all of these were done early in Harper's new administration.

I was still reeling from the fact that no political party, other than the Greens, had demanded an inquiry into how the head of the RCMP was allowed to directly interfere in the 2006 election.

93

RCMP Commissioner Giuliano Zaccardelli had violated standard protocol, issuing a press release to confirm an investigation into the Liberal decision not to tax income trusts and into NDP allegations that the then finance minister Ralph Goodale had leaked the information, leading to insider trading.

Within months after the election, the RCMP investigation found a junior bureaucrat guilty of making $6,000 as a result of his advance knowledge. Goodale was not involved and the crime amounted to small change. There was nothing more to it. .

The only investigation to take place into the outrageous RCMP interference in the election campaign was by the Commission for Public Complaints against the RCMP. Commissioner Paul Kennedy confirmed that the issuing of the media release, right before Christmas 2005, appeared to have had an immediate and long-lasting impact on public opinion, giving Stephen Harper his minority win. The Commission for Public Complaints lacked subpoena powers and thus Zaccardelli was never subjected to questioning. He declined to provide any explanation voluntarily and was appointed to a nice gig in Rome with Interpol. Had Canada become a banana republic overnight? Where was the outrage?

Everything since then has accelerated the concentration of power in the office of the prime minister. The degree of partisanship, the total control of MPs within caucuses, and the use of attack ads and ad hominem attacks have grown like Topsy.

By May 2006 I was no longer an observer to politics from the outside. I had taken the plunge. It was personally high risk. If I did not win the leadership, I would have to find a job for which partisan affiliation with the Green Party was not a permanent stigma. It would mean that I could not return to the environmental movement. I was a single mother with a fifteen-year-old daughter. It was a competitive race with a national tour, debates, and a major leadership convention set for late August. My daughter was supportive. We both knew what was at stake and decided to take the chance. She was at my side when the votes were announced and I was declared leader with over 60 per cent of the vote.

Within months of my becoming leader of the Green Party, Stéphane Dion won leadership of the Liberal Party. The new era of manipulation through pre-emptive campaigns of character assassination began within weeks with Conservative attack ads ridiculing Dion. He was denigrated not for his policies, but in an unfair smear, for his character. The electoral version of a shock-and-awe campaign began in January 2007—more than a year and a half before the next election. It was the first time in Canadian political history that television time had been purchased for campaign-style advertising outside an electoral writ period. Elections Canada has still not come up with spending limits for political parties during non-election times. I doubt anyone had ever anticipated that a party would buy advertising outside election time.

Harper's promises of transparency and a high standard of ethical behaviour were clearly kiboshed. He reversed his election platform and taxed income trusts, passed a fixed election date law, and then smashed it to claim electoral advantage by calling an election on September 7, 2008. He even managed to remove the "duty to act honestly" for his cabinet members and senior civil servants, present in the previous code of ethics, in the new Accountability Act. His campaign pledges were in tatters.

The increase in nastiness and hyper-partisanship in the House of Commons became apparent as well. As leader of the Green Party, but still without a seat in the House, I attended Question Period as often as possible and watched from the galleries. Former speaker Peter Milliken had kindly accepted my request that, as leader of a federal political party, I be allowed a reserved spot in the Diplomatic Gallery. Having experienced Question Period in the 1980s (not just on television, but up close and personal), I was shocked by the deliberately vicious line of talking points and responses of the new regime.

When I made this point to *Globe and Mail* columnist Jeffrey Simpson, he dismissed it, reminding me of how the "Rat Pack" of former Liberal MPs John Nunziata, Sheila Copps, Don Boudria, and Brian Tobin had behaved. I pointed out that their antics only received note because they were unusual. In today's context, the Rat Pack would not get noticed at all. Who would hear them above the noise?

In the past, exchanges in the House had been unscripted and sometimes witty, and, while frequently unhelpful, at least answers were generally related to the topic. Now things were very different indeed. Any question was used by the Conservatives as an excuse to attack the questioner.

I was in my seat in the Diplomatic Gallery in Question Period when former Liberal leader Stéphane Dion asked about the allegations that Afghan detainees were turned over to local authorities even though our military knew their fate would likely be torture. Stephen Harper responded by attacking Dion. Harper alleged Dion cared more about the Taliban than about Canadian soldiers. Harper's words hit me as if they were a physical blow. I felt the air expressed from my lungs from the shock.

No members of parliament in other Canadian political parties had ever used opposition questions as an opportunity to attack the questioner's motives, allegiances, or patriotism. Yet now it was routine. If any MP suggested concern about abusing the Charter of Rights and Freedoms through harsh measures, mandatory minimums proven to be ineffective in other countries, then that member was attacked as caring more about criminals than about innocent victims of crime. Concerned about invasions of privacy under new internet snooping laws? Clearly, you are more concerned with the rights of child pornographers than with innocent Canadians. Concerned about the risk of catastrophic oil spills on the BC coastline? Then you must be anti-Canadian, against the national interest in pipelines to reach new markets.

When questioned, attack. When asked for the evidence, attack.

Attack anyone in the House of Commons who is not a member of the Conservative Party.

These "take no prisoners" bare-fisted tactics were a direct threat to a healthy, respectful Westminster parliamentary democracy.

Branding exercises became paramount as the new administration insisted on calling itself "Canada's New Government" and demanded that civil servants do the same. Following the 2011 election, the messaging became more personal. "Canada's New Government" was replaced with "the Harper Government," a term that in Westminster parliamentary tradition is absurd. It remains Canada's government, composed of an executive organized by the prime minister and a loyal opposition. All these parts operate as Parliament, and it is Parliament to whom the prime minister is accountable. No more. Now it is branded the Harper government and all other MPs are ostracized from any meaningful role.

As leader of the Green Party, from 2006 to the fall election of 2008 I worked to raise issues from the sidelines. Without a seat in the House, I found the effort to address climate change and other issues was more than daunting.

We had not been expecting a fall election. Stephen Harper had brought in legislation to fix the election date, so no election was expected for at least another two years. Although in a minority parliament there is always a chance that the opposition will vote non-confidence, bring down the government, and provoke an election, it seemed unlikely that the prime minister would break his own fixed election date law. Rumours that he might do so were fuelled by a TV advertising blitz from the Conservative Party, featuring a kinder, gentler Stephen Harper. The ads featured him, wearing a sweater vest, with his family.

By Labour Day 2008, the political pundits sensed an election in the air. I was spending a lot of time in Guelph to help a strong Green by-election campaign there with voting day set for Monday,

September 8. Meanwhile, my daughter, Victoria Cate, started grade twelve. Unbeknownst to me, she went to every teacher and said, "If Stephen Harper drops the writ, I won't be back." She had decided her priority was to be with me should the election be called in the fall. Victoria Cate was prepared to lose the chance of graduating with her friends and instead complete high school the following year. When she joined me in Guelph on the weekend, she shared the news. I was at first overwhelmed by her loyalty and commitment, but horrified that she was prepared to lose a year of school. Then before I could argue the point, she told me her teachers and guidance counsellor had found a solution. They all supported her decision, but told her to return whenever the election was over and pick up her courses as best she could.

Sure enough, Harper broke his fixed election date law, calling an election for the day after Thanksgiving. We rode the crazy roller coaster of a federal election campaign together. As in 2006, the NDP campaign targeted the Liberals, attacking Dion's "Green Shift" climate plan. The plan was quite similar to the Green Party approach. Sadly, the campaign itself never allowed for a real discussion on climate. Had the events of the fall of 2008 been a major extreme weather event, the focus might have stayed on the climate. As it turned out, the major event was the financial crisis. Even though I was the only leader in the televised leaders' debate to point out that Canada was already in recession—with Stephen Harper saying, "If we were going to be in a recession, we would be in one already"—the campaign focussed on economic concerns.

The strategies were managed by the backrooms of each party with the cynical techniques of message control and image over substance. The news media, as has become all too typical, covered the campaign as if it were a horse race.

98   The 2008 election results—another Conservative minority— were almost immediately followed by a major crisis in Harper's control of Parliament. The November economic statement, and its incredible claim that the federal budget would remain in surplus

over the coming five years, was made even more controversial by the announced plan to eliminate the per vote subsidy. The per vote subsidy was part of a major overhaul of Canada's election spending and financing rules brought in by former prime minister Jean Chrétien in 2004. Suddenly we went from the certainty of a minority parliament with Stephen Harper as prime minister to the prospect of a coalition government of Liberals and New Democrats, with the Bloc Québécois on the sidelines as a silent partner.

And then Stephen Harper did the unthinkable. The low point of our democracy was his decision to shut down Parliament to avoid a confidence vote he was sure to lose.

Ronald Wright, author of numerous bestsellers, including his Massey lecture, *A Short History of Progress*—and in one of life's lovelier developments, now one of my bosses, as a constituent of Saanich–Gulf Islands—wrote the following letter to the *Globe and Mail*:

> Modern parliamentary democracy rests on a single great principle: The government must have the consent of the governed. This consent is delegated by the people to their MPs. The government must then be able to carry the "confidence" of the House of Commons. Majority governments rarely lose that confidence; minority governments often do. When the government cannot carry the House, it falls.
>
> Suspending Parliament to dodge a vote the government fears it will lose is so deeply undemocratic it should never have been mooted by politicians, the media or the Governor General. The English Civil War was fought on this very issue—after King Charles I shut down Parliament when he found its restrictions uncongenial. The King lost his head.
>
> We no longer behead people in Canada, but Stephen Harper's *coup d'état* cannot be allowed to stand, not least because of the precedent. Any future government can now slip the leash of democracy in the same way. This is how constitutions fail.[1]

99

Constitutional law expert Errol Mendes of the University of Ottawa warned, "This is a major constitutional precedent and that worries me more than anything else... Any time the prime minister wants to evade the confidence of the House, now he can use this precedent to do so."[2]

Former commissioner of official languages Keith Spicer was blunter: "Finally the world pays a little attention to Canada. And what does it see? Zimbabwe run by the Queen."[3]

Sure enough, a little more than one year later, and Errol Mendes's prediction that the 2008 prorogation would serve to allow any prime minister (in this case, the same prime minister) to do it again was fulfilled with a second prorogation.

The prime minister claimed his bills were not moving through the Senate. Well, they were, but he had just shut down the House and the Senate, and all bills, good and bad, had to go back to scratch and start over. By the time Stephen Harper prorogued the third time, even though his third prorogation met the time-worn tradition of setting out a new agenda through the Speech from the Throne, Canadians no longer believed him. The pattern was established and we had begun to notice.

It was also increasingly difficult to access information. Our freedom of information laws seem to have morphed into freedom *from* information. In global rankings for transparency and access to information, Canada plummeted to fifty-first in the world, behind Colombia, Niger, and Angola. The survey published by the Centre for Law and Democracy noted that Canada's thirty-year-old law is languishing behind those of other countries and needs modernization.

Certainly, my access requests as an MP are frequently met with requests for time extensions. It's like pulling teeth to get information that should be readily available. Ironically, the single job category in the federal civil service that has grown substantially—by 15 per cent—under Stephen Harper is for what are described as "information officers." I can only conclude that the title is Orwellian and their job is to ensure that only the "official story" is released.

As in the Monty Python sketch, Canadian democracy was nailed to its little perch in hopes the public would not notice the resemblance to a dead parrot. Something drastic was required to revive it. The first step was surely to point out what democracy, specifically a Westminster parliamentary democracy, looks like. In a parliamentary democracy, the prime minister serves at the pleasure of Parliament, not the other way around.

Our system is not supposed to look like a dictatorship. It does not involve central control by a prime minister's office. It does not involve non-stop partisan campaigning in a permanent state of heightened electoral warfare in the absence of governing. Democracy should look a lot like the people who elected their government. And those in government should make decisions based on the best evidence available—not on focus groups and polls, but on empirical evidence, scientific understanding balanced and assessed in the public interest. Before the 2011 election, it was the excess partisanship of Parliament that worried me. But following the 2011 election of a majority of Conservative MPs, Stephen Harper had the power to do what no previous prime minister had ever done: declare war on science and evidence running contrary to his desired policy.

Hostage to Political Minority

If in the U.S. the executive and the legislative branches are deadlocked, in Canada the executive has almost wholly consumed the legislature: the prime minister is "responsible" to Parliament only in the most formalistic sense. What we are left with, as the political scientist Peter Russell has put it, is a presidential system, without the Congress. (The Americans, perhaps, have a parliamentary system without a prime minister.)

Two systems, both dysfunctional, in opposing ways. Is there nevertheless a common thread between the two? I think there is. Both have become hostage to small groups of voters, the objects of vastly disproportionate amounts of the parties' time and attention. In both, the parties are sharply divided on regional lines. And in both, politics has become increasingly, corrosively nasty. I suggest these trends are not accidental, but have to do with a feature the two share: the first past the post electoral system.

The most important thing to know about first past the post is that it is highly leveraged: Not only do the parties' representation in the legislature bear no resemblance to their respective shares. of the popular vote, but tiny swings in the vote lead to exponentially larger swings in electoral outcomes.

Finding and mobilizing those votes are thus a matter of huge consequence to the parties. In Canada, these are typically the swing voters, the uncommitted and disengaged; in the more polarized politics of the U.S., it is more a matter of "ginning up the base," motivating your most committed—and therefore demanding—supporters to get out to vote.

So where our politics has converged on the centre, theirs is increasingly dominated by the fringes. But in both, politics has become less and less about the broad public interest, more and more focussed on appealing to a small fraction of the electorate. Some votes really are worth a great deal more than others . . .

In this fevered, divided atmosphere, is it any wonder that politics has become so nasty? With so much riding on so few votes, the parties are in a state of almost permanent hysteria. If anything, that's even more true in our system. Depending on how the vote splits, you can win a "majority" with as little as 37 per cent of the vote, heavily concentrated in one part of the country or another. Winner take all.

Suppose instead we had a system where every vote counted equally; where it was in every party's interest to campaign in every part of the country; where you worked to expand your base gradually, rather than in accidental jags; where the possibility of winning over supporters of other parties entered into the equation, rather than just enraging your own.

Suppose, that is, that both countries started to realize their politics had become radically dysfunctional, not so much because of their parties or systems but the incentives facing their politicians. And suppose they decided to do something about it.

ANDREW COYNE[4]

Chapter Six

SCIENCE
UNDER ATTACK

ITTING ON THE edge of the Salish Sea, at a waterfront café in the beautiful little town where I live, Sidney by the Sea, I was reeling from the description of the slaughter of science going on in the Department of Fisheries and Oceans (DFO). It was not news that the Harper administration seemed to have declared war on science, particularly research related to nature and the impacts of human activities. It was spring 2014, and Canada had endured three years of Stephen Harper's blitzkrieg against environmental policy, made possible by the majority he had held since the 2011 election. I had been elected member of parliament representing Saanich–Gulf Islands, a riding comprising the Saanich Peninsula and numerous islands in the Salish Sea, the defining marine ecosystem of the riding.

Prominent and respected Canadian scientist Dr. Peter Ross was telling me why he was moving to Vancouver. As sailboats bobbed on the blue waters of the Salish Sea and the snow on Mount Baker glimmered in the sunlight, he told me of the loss of his entire program. The marine contaminants program had been eliminated, and the eighty scientists from across Canada who worked within it had been terminated. Luckily for Canada, Dr. Ross was snapped up by the Vancouver Aquarium to direct its research into ocean pollution. Otherwise, like so many terminated government scientists, he could have left for a more science-friendly country.

"There will be no more government monitoring of contamination to our oceans—not on the BC coast or any coast. We will have no studies of what kinds of pollution are reaching the ocean, nor how it impacts marine life," he said. "There will be no more research."

Instead, he told me the DFO budget would include $1.2 million for the department to go out and buy the information. "But who will be collecting the information for the government to buy?" I asked. "Does Harper think this kind of information can be found on Google?"

Although in modern times, sound science has been the bulwark of sensible government policy, it was not always so. Before the separation of church and state, the apparatus of the state could be used to sanction any scientist whose work was seen as a threat to the prevailing faith-based systems. We like to think those days are gone, but there may be a new state religion threatening science.

In the seventeenth century, one of the most prominent examples of such a scientist was Galileo. His scientific inquiry put him in conflict with the state, and he spent the last years of his life under house arrest after the Catholic Church convicted him of "vehement suspicion of heresy." His crime was that he supported the theory, first put forward by Copernicus, that the Earth revolved around the Sun, not the other way around.

Galileo died in 1642, and, over time, science has become deeply embedded in public policy. The Age of Enlightenment initiated a steady retreat of superstition. Since then, there has been a growing acceptance of science and evidence-based decision making as hallmarks of modern democracies.

Every now and then, however, some anti-science fad will arise, as in some U.S. states where Creationism is taught as a theory competing with evolution.

Government policy requires that evidence be based on verifiable, independent science. For over a hundred years, Canadian government scientists have collected data, conducted experiments, carried out research, and advised politicians. In fact, the first of Canada's scientific institutes, the Geological Survey of Canada, was founded in 1842, before Confederation. Whole departments of our government particularly depend on science—environment, fisheries and oceans, agriculture, health. Although increasingly governments accept industry-sourced packages of scientific data, it is essential that qualified independent government scientists review and analyze the industry evidence.

Sometimes government scientists make mistakes. The collapse of the North Atlantic cod fishery was overwhelmingly due to federally set catch rates that exceeded the cod population's ability to recover. The Department of Fisheries and Oceans believed so passionately in their theoretical models of "spawning biomass" for setting annual allowable catch rates for cod that they ignored dissenting scientists, such as the late Ransom Myers, a heroic DFO scientist, and dismissed the protests of the in-shore fishermen in the traditional fisheries conducted closer to shore. It was the off-shore draggers who were doing the lion's share of the damage and who wielded the most political clout. DFO scientists refused to listen to the warnings that the cod were disappearing, and politicians were equally impervious to the warnings. The scientists believed that cod were too plentiful to disappear, and politicians wanted to keep all the fish plants open. The "commercial extinction" of the cod, as Fisheries Minister Brian Tobin would eventually describe it, was a preventable tragedy and is one of the planet's most appalling stories of human destruction of a populous animal species, as well as the thirty thousand jobs that depended upon it.

Sometimes government scientists were wrong in failing to assess a toxic chemical. Canadian government scientists never agreed with the U.S. EPA that Agent Orange was an unsafe product. It was never banned in Canada but ceased to be available for legal use when there were no longer any stocks of 2,4,5-T, which constituted 50 per cent of the Agent Orange mixture, as a result of action in the U.S.

The regulatory errors have been even more notorious. Approval of thalidomide to help expectant mothers with morning sickness was one such tragedy. It led to more and better testing and regulation in many countries. Governments and their scientists are supposed to learn from their mistakes. And sometimes they do.

Industry lobbyists can influence government decisions. The tobacco industry's determined efforts to deny the health threats of smoking, battling the advice of the medical community and the U.S. Surgeon General, is well known. One of the most shameful episodes is less known: the seventy-year battle to ban lead in gasoline. Dr. Alice Walker, the founder of public health policy in the United States, argued in the 1920s when lead as a gas additive was first proposed that it would be a betrayal of public health to allow it. Her concerns were overruled when the car industry made a direct appeal on the floor of Congress to the economic impact of a new and powerful fleet of cars to take Americans faster and farther. "See the USA in your Chevrolet" was presented as a call akin to manifest destiny.

In the 1970s, a prominent Harvard University Medical School scientist, Dr. Herbert Needleman, conducted research demonstrating a link between lead levels in the teeth of inner city children and lower IQ. When other researchers attacked him, Harvard University failed to defend him. Although it was never revealed who funded the researchers who claimed Needleman's work was invalid, it was suspected that the lead industry played a role. Needleman moved his career to the less prestigious University of Pittsburgh. Largely thanks to his work on the loss of intellectual capacity for a whole generation of inner city children, lead was finally banned as a gasoline additive in Canada and the U.S. One astonishing recent scientific study suggests that another side effect of lead in gasoline was a rise in violent crime. Since the banning of lead in gas, the rate of violent crime has fallen dramatically in cities throughout North America—all in lockstep with each other, but with a very large range of difference in city strategies to fight crime. Had policy makers listened to medical experts, the evidence suggests deaths caused by crimes of violence would have been avoided. As Dr. Needleman argued in a 2005 paper, lead builds up in the brain in a place that triggers violence.[1]

There are many such examples of profit motives overriding public health protection. Manufacturers in both the U.S. and Canada always try to some degree to influence the government decisions, but the influence of manufacturers—especially giant multinationals—on regulatory decisions has increased.

There will always be areas of scientific uncertainty, which presents challenges to public policy makers. In the face of uncertainty, the best approach is to exercise the precautionary principle. Essentially, that means look both ways before crossing a street. Where there are risks, minimize exposure for the most vulnerable. And constantly try to improve upon your foundation of knowledge to reduce uncertainties.

Government scientific research is important because it is—ideally—independent of commercial interest. For the sake of open and unfettered scientific knowledge, scientists can, for example, explore the changes found in freshwater lakes as a result of acid rain or the buildup of dioxins in gulls' eggs. Although commercial or academic researchers could do this work, the consistent maintenance of information, lack of bias or conflict of interest, open access to the research, and ability to concentrate on areas requiring information for policy makers make government science indispensable. Government science plays a critical role in developing evidence-based public policy.

As policy makers began to assess the extraordinary levels of complexity in climate science, it became clear that an extra effort would be required for non-scientists to stay on top of the emerging evidence.

Climate science deals with complex relationships within and between the atmosphere, land masses, and oceans and their nearly infinite interactions. Climate science includes paleoclimatology, which tries to reconstruct the climate of hundreds, thousands, and even millions of years ago through fossil evidence and proxies for warming and carbon—for example, from snail shells and fossilized pollen. Scientists search through the records of human history for evidence, where it exists, of temperatures in the air and the ocean.

Climate science includes those who assess the chemistry of the oceans, monitoring how the carbon dioxide in the atmosphere is mixing with the surface of the ocean and converting to carbonic acid. It includes biologists monitoring the disappearance of species because of climate-induced loss of habitat. And it includes glaciologists collecting data from thousands of millennia found in Antarctic ice cores or assessing the rate of the disappearance of glaciers. Freshwater scientists, soil scientists—virtually no discipline is irrelevant.

Climate science includes the modellers, who run giant computer models that attempt to replicate the planet's interacting systems to assess how climate will be affected by rising levels of carbon dioxide. It includes physicists using satellite data to measure the gravitational pull of continents and, through that, inferentially, to measure the declining weight of the Antarctic and Greenland ice masses.

Strangely to some, climate science does not include meteorologists. The people who try to predict when it will next rain are, ironically, disinclined to believe climate scientists. Some, but not all, cannot imagine climate scientists' ability to model how rising GHG will impact the planet in a hundred years, when they cannot get next week right. It leads to the maddening newscast with the predictable "Mother Nature just threw us a curve ball … "

All of the research from thousands of researchers appears in peer-reviewed scientific journals. The available research, even in the late 1980s, numbered in the thousands of publications.

To help politicians understand the complex interdisciplinary science of climate change, the Intergovernmental Panel on Climate Change (IPCC) was created in 1988. The over two thousand scientists on the IPCC are appointed by governments. By definition, their consensus excludes research that suggests the climate crisis is worse than the consensus, just as it excludes research that suggests there may be less impact. It is, in other words, by its very structure and mandate, a conservative body. And it is cumbersome. The reports to policy makers come out only every five or six years. The first assessment was in 1990, the next not until 1995, the third in 2001, the fourth in 2007, and the fifth in 2014. As a result, by the time the reports are published, new evidence has, every single time, made it clear the report has underestimated the threat.

Still, the industry-funded climate change denier movement has taken aim at the IPCC. Any error, no matter how insignificant, found in reports covering hundreds of topic areas and numbering thousands of pages is seized upon as though the IPCC has been "discredited."

Meanwhile, the fossil fuel propaganda machine has become very sophisticated in suggesting plausible storylines to undermine the science. The key to instilling doubt about climate science is to start with something true and morph it into something inaccurate.

For example, it is true that the greenhouse effect is perfectly natural. Without those heat-trapping gases (water vapour, carbon, methane, and so on) Planet Earth would be too cold to sustain human life. It is true that carbon dioxide is a trace gas. It is 25 per cent of the natural greenhouse effect. But it is not true to make what seems a logical leap and to say carbon dioxide is a tiny part of global warming about which we shouldn't be concerned.

The natural greenhouse effect is largely water vapour, but 111 water vapour is only on the rise because of warming triggered by the increased levels of carbon dioxide. Carbon dioxide from burning fossil fuels is rapidly increasing.

To assess the relative contribution to global warming from different gases, it is not enough to know the volume emitted in any one year. We must also understand how long that gas remains in the atmosphere. The lifetime for carbon in the atmosphere is around one hundred years; water vapour, about ten days. One of Canada's leading experts in climate science, Dr. Gordon McBean, puts it this way:

> The 100 years means that it is not what you put in this year, but how much did you put in, as a country for example, over the past 100 years. Although China is the largest emitter now, the OECD countries have caused about 80 per cent of the observed increase. So when we address emission reductions, we should factor this in—"common but differentiated responsibilities" according to the Climate Convention.
>
> Think of it as a bank account. If you and friends had put in most of the money over the past 100 years, would somebody else be able to take out more just because they put in the most last year? [2]

Climate deniers have an easy time injecting doubt by asking, "How would we know carbon dioxide has increased? No one kept records even five hundred years ago and scientists are making claims about thousands of years." It is easily explained, once you know the science.

Data obtained from the analysis of Antarctic ice cores give us a high-tech, modern body of evidence of carbon dioxide concentrations in the atmosphere going back hundreds of thousands of years. Ice never freezes completely solid. Modern science can ascertain when ice froze—ten thousand years ago, two hundred thousand years ago, and so on. Each air bubble is like a time capsule of the planet's atmosphere on that date. That is how we know with certainty that over the last million years the atmosphere has never had a higher concentration of carbon dioxide than 280 parts per million. Until the last several decades. In 2013, carbon dioxide crossed the 400 parts per million threshold and continues to climb.[3]

Because the isotype ratios of human-emitted fossil fuel carbon are different from those of natural carbon (such as the carbon emitted from decaying trees), scientists are now able to distinguish these two types of carbon and have been able to establish with certainty that most of the growth in global concentrations of carbon, on the order of 80 per cent, is due to pollution.

Statements pooh-poohing climate science are often based on a completely false notion of the chronology. It was simply not the case that scientists observed rising temperature levels, higher sea level and storm surges, more droughts, more dangerous and more frequent extreme events, floods, fires, and storms, and then started trying to fit some facts to a new hypothesis. In fact, in the late 1890s a paper setting out the threat to the global climate from emitting greenhouse gases was written by Svante Arrhenius, the Swedish scientist who won a Nobel Prize for his work on the physical chemistry of acids and bases. He also wrote a paper stating that increased amounts of carbon in the atmosphere threatened to destabilize the climate.[4] But even Arrhenius was not the first to put forth this argument. An 1824 paper by French mathematician Fourier made the same points.[5]

Scientists didn't "invent" the theory that carbon pollution leads to global warming to explain observed impacts. The chemical properties of carbon and the nature of our atmosphere made the threat obvious decades, even a century, before it materialized.

I could not doubt the connection between rising greenhouse gases and climate change because the observed aberrations, the dramatic change in our weather patterns, fit the 1980s Environment Canada predictions like a glove. The climate models presented in 1986–88 to the minister of environment were driven only by expected increases in greenhouse gases, and before significant climate changes were actually observed. They only failed to the extent that the damage from human-caused global warming was occurring faster and the impact, worse.

I have had a ringside seat for over twenty-five years as the scientific community first warned about a future problem and then watched it unfold in ways that fit their projections, but that were more rapid and more dangerous. I have had the excruciating experience of listening to scientists while it seemed no one else was listening.

Following the awarding of the 2006 Nobel Peace Prize to Al Gore and the IPCC, if anything, things became worse. The IPCC found itself under a microscope. No doubt more scrupulous editing could have avoided some of the tempest-in-a-teapot controversies, as the media jumped on minor issues and magnified them in the public eye.

Nowhere on earth has the attack on science been as comprehensive as in Harper's administration in Canada. Governmental science has been steadily dismantled. The litany of critical research activities, laboratories and programs, and legislated mandates to maintain our knowledge that have been cut is long, and it continues to grow.

One of Stephen Harper's first actions after he became prime minister was to remove a key IPCC graph from Environment Canada's website. Although the Conservatives had carefully skirted any direct reference to their attitude toward Kyoto and climate science in the election campaign, it was clear from a fundraising letter signed by Stephen Harper before 2006 that he was vehemently opposed to Kyoto. In the letter, Kyoto is referred to as a "socialist scheme to suck money out of wealth-producing nations," and the science is described as "tentative and contradictory." Harper displayed a lack of understanding of the threat of global warming, complaining Kyoto "focuses on carbon dioxide, which is essential to life, rather than upon pollutants."[6]

In the 2005–6 election campaign, only one group managed to get Harper's Conservatives on the record on climate science.

It was a Fraser Institute kissing-cousin and climate-denier group, the Montreal Economic Institute. In response to its questionnaire, the Conservatives said they did not accept the IPCC consensus, and especially not the so-called hockey stick graph.[7] The graph was dubbed the "hockey stick" as the rapid increase in temperature shown in the graph looks like a hockey stick, rising sharply. Sure enough, soon after the election, the IPCC science was pulled from the government website.

The most outrageous of the media-fuelled controversies designed to discredit climate science was the illegal computer hacking at the Climatic Research Unit (CRU) of the University of East Anglia. The timing of the explosive accusations was meticulously planned to undermine global public confidence in climate science just as the Copenhagen climate talks opened in December 2009.

At COP11 in 2005 in Montreal, the fifteenth COP set for 2009 in Copenhagen had been established as the deadline for a next phase of Kyoto and more comprehensive climate action. Just as there are good cops and bad cops on police TV dramas, so there are good COPs and bad COPs in climate talks. Montreal was the last good COP, and Copenhagen was a very bad COP indeed. It was a complete train wreck, setting back climate action by at least a decade.

In the lead-up to Copenhagen, the media eagerly covered an alleged scandal, dubbed "climate-gate." In the Watergate scandal, the burglars were understood to be the bad guys. In the so-called climate-gate scandal, the burglars were victorious and the victims were pilloried. The director of the CRU at East Anglia, Dr. Phil Jones, stepped down pending investigation. Things looked bad. Before defending or condemning the scientists accused of fudging data, I decided I had better read all of the emails. I wish others had done so. Even my hero, journalist George Monbiot, distanced himself from Dr. Jones and called for his resignation without even reading the emails.

115

I read all three thousand email messages, more than fourteen hundred pages. It took a couple of days. I printed them out and carried them with me, reading them on airplanes and in Green Party council meetings. (It is fortunate that I can do two things at once, though reading through a stack of hundreds of pages of emails did not assure other Green Party council members that I was actually interested in the party budget.)

Amid the science were cheery notes of "need to get this surgery over and then I will get busy with my review," "getting married, did I mention, will work on this next data set as soon as I am back from my honeymoon... " The dedication evident in the messages was striking. The emails were sent right up to Christmas Eve and resumed before Boxing Day was over. These guys worked with hardly a break.

The hackers exposed the personal lives of a handful of thoroughly decent, previously anonymous scientists. Messages they never thought any stranger would see were published by thieves, following an illegal break-in and posted on a Russian server. Yet no one was calling for the thieves to be apprehended. Instead, virtual lynch mobs were forming to attack the victims of the hacking, who started getting death threats.

All the most intimate details of their lives—wives with cancer, the birth of a first grandchild—were suddenly public, and their reputations were shredded. As I mentioned earlier, I enjoyed reading the emails. The CRU at East Anglia focussed on paleoclimatology, one of the most difficult research areas. Unlike the measurement of carbon dioxide in Antarctic ice cores, a precise matter of high-tech chemical analysis of air bubbles, paleoclimatology is subject to judgment calls.

How should the science extrapolate evidence of several-hundred-year-old tree rings from one part of the planet to conditions elsewhere? The nature of the evidence is that it was often collected for another purpose.

For example, the only reason we have detailed measurements of ocean water temperature from hundreds of years ago is that the British Navy kept records in order to use ocean water in steam-room engines. Researchers struggled with assessing how the temperatures should be recalibrated when the Navy moved from wooden buckets to canvas ones.

Measurements of tree-ring growth were not being kept to help future climate scientists. So to assess what the climate was like, working inferentially from tree rings in different parts of the planet, the CRU had to exercise professional judgment. With deciduous tree rings in one place (with only seasonal photosynthesis) and coniferous tree rings (with year-round photosynthesis) in another, how should the data be presented? Reconstructing past climate from partial evidence is difficult. The scientists' shared thought process, which acknowledged the imperfect nature of their work, was fascinating. In the hands of Big Carbon's spin machine, technical jargon like "hide the decline" was torqued as though climate scientists were cooking the books.

The media and the climate deniers acted as though every bit of climate information in the hands of governments had been developed by this one group—a group they now alleged was discredited.

The emails were extremely well written, especially considering the medium. In all those email messages, not once did I spot a grammatical error. And not once was there any suggestion of fudging the science.

Over the years, the email messages reflected a dawning awareness that the scientists were being ensnared by a sting operation. Colleagues of the East Anglia scientists from around the world, including Canada, the U.S., and Europe, began to realize, rather slowly at first, that requests for information and the increased number of freedom of information applications were not from scientists. The escalating demands for their original data and background computations were attempts to entrap them, to provoke them into saying, "No, I won't give you my data," or at least to waste vast quantities of their time. Here is an excerpt from a December 2, 2008, email written when the scientists had begun to suspect that their science was being treated as a political target. 117

Message from Gavin Schmidt at NASA

To Ben Santer at Lawrence Livermore National Laboratory, copied to Phil Jones at East Anglia and others:

Ben, there are two very different things going on here. One is technical and related to the actual science and the actual statistics, the second is political, and is much more concerned with how incidents like this can be portrayed. The second is the issue here...

Thus any increase in publicity on this—whether in the pages of *Nature* or elsewhere—is much more likely to bring further negative fallout despite your desire to clear the air. Whatever you say, it will still be presented as you hiding data.

The contrarians have found that there is actually no limit to what you can ask people for (raw data, intermediate steps, additional calculations, sensitivity calculations, all the code, a workable version of the code on any platform, etc.) and like Somali pirates they have found that once someone has paid up, they can always shake them down again.[8]

He went on to suggest that the university and program directors just point out where the data can be found in the public domain and urge their questioners to try their own calculations (if they have the competence). He suggested they indicate how the calculations can be done by getting a grad student to work up the data from public sources that the contrarians keep demanding.

Eventually, three separate reviews and inquiries from different academic and government bodies concluded what I had: there was absolutely no evidence that the East Anglia scientists cherry-picked data, distorted science, or shaped information to fit a theory.

The all-party Science and Technology Committee of the UK Parliament reached this conclusion:

The focus on Professor Jones and CRU has been largely misplaced... On the much cited phrases in the leaked e-mails—"trick" and "hiding the decline"—the Committee considers that they were colloquial terms used in private e-mails and the balance of evidence is that they were not part of a systematic attempt to mislead. Insofar as the Committee was able to consider accusations of dishonesty against CRU, the Committee considers that there is no case to answer.[9]

The East Anglia group was completely exonerated and Dr. Jones was reinstated, but, as so often happens when someone is accused of wrongdoing (think of the accusations against Ralph Goodale in the 2005–6 election), the news of exoneration was buried in the back pages, whereas the accusations had been front-page news, above the fold. To this day, the occasional media story will refer to "leaked" emails instead of stolen emails. To this day, accusations are made that there was something fishy in the East Anglia science. Mark Twain had it right: A lie makes its way halfway round the world while the truth is lacing up its boots.

How does science survive once targeted by Big Carbon, with hundreds of millions of dollars in propaganda campaigns designed to undermine the research, to create doubt? Another Monty Python line comes to mind: "No one expects the Spanish Inquisition." Especially not a bunch of people who have chosen for their life's work the pursuit of knowledge for its own sake.

The mainstream media in Canada and the United States rarely probe the source of the many disinformation campaigns within the so-called climate controversy. A rare example was the January 21, 2010, issue of *Rolling Stone*. In the wake of the disastrous Copenhagen climate conference, most of its cover page was taken up with "YOU IDIOTS" in red, along with the subtitle: "Meet the Planet's Worst Enemies."[10] That article in *Rolling Stone* is one of the few publications—and among the best—covering the millions being spent in defence of fossil fuels through deliberate distortion of climate science.

Rarely do journalists follow the money to find those who are bankrolling anti-climate science propaganda. *Rolling Stone* targeted Rupert Murdoch, Warren Buffett, and flip-floppers in Congress. But they are pikers compared with the Koch brothers. Kansas-based Charles and David Koch, brothers and owners of a vast fossil fuel empire, have donated tens of millions to propaganda campaigns to block climate action. Although most of their activity has been in the U.S., the Koch brothers have also made generous donations to right-wing organizations in Canada, such as the Fraser Institute, to promote their interests.[11]

It is estimated that a half a billion dollars has been spent in the industry campaign to stop governments from taking action to protect our children's futures.

Science has never been exposed to such a concerted, well-financed campaign of derision. Big Carbon has even trumped the Vatican's assault on Galileo.[12]

As industry-funded assaults on climate science proliferated around the world, in Canada, Stephen Harper continued dismantling government science.

The position of science advisor to the prime minister was eliminated in 2008. By 2012, the National Round Table on the Environment and the Economy (NRTEE) was also eliminated. Although not a research body, it was the last governmental advisory body on science, nature, or sustainable economics. Ironically, after Brian Mulroney established the NRTEE, its existence was used as an excuse to eliminate the Science Council, the Canadian Environmental Advisory Council, and the Economic Council. When Harper killed the NRTEE, his environment minister, Peter Kent, said it had been rendered unnecessary by the advent of the internet.

March 2012 marked the end of all funding for the Canadian Foundation for Climate and Atmospheric Sciences (now the Canadian Climate Forum). The funds put in place in 2000, $110 million over ten years for autonomous research funding in Canada's major universities, had been spent expanding our understanding of the climate crisis in its multi-faceted disciplines of inquiry.

top My first press conference, with my mom and Nobel laureates, including Linus Pauling. Washington, 1960.

above My mom, me, Senator Eugene McCarthy, and my brother, Geoffrey. U.S. Senate, Washington, DC, spring 1965.

above Bottle-feeding my lamb Corey. Bloomfield, Connecticut, spring 1966.

above Paul Newman and me at the Democratic National Convention. (I am wearing a paper dress with Eugene McCarthy's image.) Chicago, August 1968.

top My mom and dad at the entrance to the Marion Elizabeth Schooner Restaurant, our family business. Margaree Harbour, Cape Breton Island, Nova Scotia, summer 1973.

above With my godfather, Cliff Robertson. Cabot Trail, Cape Breton Island, summer 1984.

top With Pete Seeger at the Fate of the Earth Conference. Ottawa, June 1986. (Photo credit: Robert Del Tredici.)

above In Speaker's Chambers. *Left to right*: Wayne McCrory, Colleen McCrory, me, Jim Fulton, Speaker John Fraser, Vicky Husband, Herb Hammond, and Erika. House of Commons, Ottawa, 1987.

top Celebrating success on the final day of negotiations for the Ozone Protocol. *Left to right*: John Hoffman, Tim Leah, me, Wayne Evans, and Vic Buxton. Montreal, September 1987.

above Kayaking in Gwaii Haanas. August 1988.

left With Gordon Lightfoot. Altamira, Brazil, February 1989.

above Sting, me, and law school classmate Peter Dalglish (founder of Street Kids International). Toronto, May 1989.

above Victoria Cate's christening, with godfather Farley Mowat and dad
Ian Burton. Baddeck, Nova Scotia, August 1991.

top At the World Women's Congress for a Healthy Planet, Victoria Cate and me with former congresswoman Bella Abzug and Vandana Shiva. Miami, Florida, November 1991.

above At the Rio Earth Summit, with former Norwegian prime minister Gro Harlem Brundtland. June 1992.

top At the Rio Earth Summit, with Désirée McGraw, Suzanna (from DFAIT), the Honourable Charles Caccia, Victoria Cate in stroller and me, and Vicky Husband. June 1992.

above "Have Baby: Will Travel," with Jane Goodall (making chimp noises to Victoria Cate's delight). Ottawa, 1993.

top With Paul McCartney and Friends of the Earth Board, Julia Langer, and Mary Granskou. Toronto, October 1991.

above Canada Day Party at my and Ian's home. *Left to right*: Dr. Digby McLaren, the Honourable John Fraser, me, Ambassador John Bell, Jim MacNeill, and Phyllis MacNeill. Ottawa, July 1, 1992.

top The Clayoquot Express arrives in Vancouver. *At right*: my mom and kilted dad. *In middle*: Victoria Cate and me. November 1993.

above Meetings of the Earth Charter Commission, "Rio plus 5," with Mikhail Gorbachev and wife Raisa, Victoria Cate, and me. Rio de Janeiro, June 1997.

right My parents and brother in our gift shop. Nova Scotia, 2000.

above Meeting at 24 Sussex Drive, with Prime Minister Paul Martin, on the protection of the Arctic National Wildlife Refuge. *Back row:* Ken Madsen (Sierra Club), Larry Bagnell (M P Yukon), Monte Hummel (World Wildlife Fund), and Glen Davis. *Front row:* me, Norma Kassi (Gwich'in Nation), Paul Martin, and David Suzuki. Ottawa, spring 2005.

above At the Montreal Climate negotiations (COP11). Backstage with
Bill Clinton and Ruth Edwards, Amelia Clarke, Faith, Geneva Guerin,
Rosa Kouri, Ashley Paige, John Bennett, Mark Lutes, Joy Kennedy,
World Council of Churches delegates from Africa and Fiji, Alden Meyer,
Morag Carter, Zoe Caron, Matthew Carroll, Sam Coren, John Streicker,
Anna-Liisa Aunio, Sarah Krinitski, Lindsay Telford, Billy Parish, Jeca
Glor-Bell, and others. December 10, 2005.

top My swearing in as member of parliament for Saanich–Gulf Islands, House of Commons, Ottawa. *Back row, left to right*: my nephew Andrew McDonald, his wife, Michaela, holding baby Grace, Craig Cantin, Ben Rankin, Sami Alwani, Jim Bennett, Jim Bruce, Sue Bates, Ruth Bruce, Winona Linn, Jim MacNeill, Clotilda Yakimchuk, Maude Mooney, Debra Eindiguer, and Nyssa McLeod. *Front row*: my stepdaughters, Jo MacArthur and Nadya Burton; me with goddaughter Mary Jane on my lap (daughter of Andrew and Michaela); and Cate May Burton. Ottawa, June 1, 2011.

above At Saanich Town Hall, a small group of constituents meet with me about a local problem following a formal meeting. September 2013.

Cuts in 2011 in Environment Canada seemed directed at anything with the word "climate" attached to it. The entire group of scientists working on research for adaptation to climate change—for example, those estimating structural stresses from greater snow loads on roofs and calculating the required changes in building codes—was laid off. The entire Adaptation to Climate Change Research Group was disbanded, as was the group within Natural Resources Canada working on Arctic ice cores. As a result, an eighty-thousand-year climate record in ice cores was abandoned. (The minister said he hoped a university with a big freezer would take the ice cores.) And the nine glaciologists who had done the work were moved to focus on other issues.

Federal funding to the Polar Environmental and Atmospheric Research Laboratory (PEARL) facility on Ellesmere Island was eliminated. As a result, the lab could no longer operate year-round, even though $10 million in state-of-the-art equipment had recently been installed. At 80 degrees north latitude, PEARL is the closest lab on the planet to the North Pole. The annual cost of running the lab was only $1.5 million, but, despite dedicating an additional $8 million for CRA to audit environmental groups, Harper's administration had no money to maintain critical research. The world's scientific community was stunned. The outrage led to the resumption of funding nearly two years later. Despite some losses due to maintenance issues, the PEARL will be able to continue operations after its near-death experience.[13]

In 2011, it was announced that the Experimental Lakes Area (ELA) near Kenora, Ontario, was to close. This facility is unique in the world. Fifty-eight freshwater lakes 250 kilometres east of Winnipeg have been the testing ground for freshwater science research since the late 1960s. Ground-breaking work on acid rain, on the link between phosphates in detergents and eutrophication (the overfertilization of aquatic systems leading to algal bloom), and on the threat of higher levels of UV (amplified as a result of the warmer waters caused by climate change)—all of these findings were made possible because the government of Canada maintained this real-world laboratory of freshwater wilderness lakes. Just a few years earlier, when Stephen Harper was already prime minister, $3 million in new investments were made to upgrade the labs. The running cost per year? Six hundred thousand dollars.

Some speculated that the ELA was targeted precisely because much of its award-winning research had been conducted by Dr. David Schindler, the scientist who established that the oil sands tailings ponds were leaking into and contaminating the Athabasca River. Schindler was a very sharp thorn in Harper's side.

Efforts to maintain the ELA by the province of Ontario and the International Institute for Sustainable Development (IISD) are under way at this writing, but all of the government scientists who were doing the research at the ELA were given layoff notices in the fall of 2013. The layoffs came with an offer to redeploy them to other work. Because the ELA is no longer managed federally, the DFO scientists with ongoing work in the ELA had to choose between continuing research at the ELA or having a job. And, for good measure, all federal core funding to the IISD—an institute created by Mulroney—has been cut.

Then there are the personnel cuts. As noted, the Department of Fisheries and Oceans has shut down its national contaminants program. Nearly all of the DFO scientists studying marine toxicology across Canada have been laid off. According to Dr. Peter Ross, "The entire pollution file for the government of Canada, and marine environment in Canada's three oceans, will be overseen by five junior biologists scattered across Canada—one of which will be in BC."[14]

All the scientists working in the fisheries habitat programs have been laid off, because the Fisheries Act has been gutted to remove habitat protection as a requirement. All the science that was conducted inside national parks has been cut.

In addition, the science libraries of the Canadian Forest Service and DFO have been shuttered. DFO has gone from having eleven to four regional libraries, and although the Conservative talking point is that the libraries are being digitalized to enhance public access, memos obtained by access to information requests confirm that much of the material is to be "culled." Scientists reported watching volumes of material being carted off to the dump. Based on my research, it appears this operation violated the legal protection of Canada's "documentary heritage" found in the Library and Archives of Canada Act.

In October 2011, Canada made news around the world when international journals realized Canadian scientists were being muzzled. The issue came to light when the internationally prestigious journal *Science,* which had published Dr. Kristi Miller's work on viruses linked to salmon aquaculture operations, had tried to arrange media interviews with Dr. Miller and the Privy Council Office ordered her to refuse.

It seems that the public outcry against muzzling scientists, including ozone and climate scientists at Environment Canada, led the Prime Minister's Office to decide the contractual arrangements with scientists were too lax. As of February 1, 2013, new rules were put in place requiring all scientists working on projects in conjunction with DFO in the Central and Arctic Region to treat all information as proprietary to DFO and, worse, to await departmental approval before submitting research to any scientific journals.

The story was broken by veteran journalist Michael Harris, in the online journal *iPolitics.* Harris has been one of the few journalists willing to dig into the pervasive repression, slashing of science, and rejection of evidence-based decision making in Harper's Ottawa.

The reaction from DFO was swift. It posted this attack on its website: "The *iPolitics* story by Michael Harris published on February 7th, 2013 is untrue. There have been no changes to the Department's publication policy."[15]

Harris recounts that he was stunned. He had verified the change with several scientists external to DFO. He called Dr. Jeff

Hutchings at Dalhousie University, who reconfirmed the changes. Then Harris received support from an unexpected source—an anonymous DFO scientist posted the email from Michelle Wheatley, the Central and Arctic science director, detailing the new publication policy.

The anonymous scientist posted, "Here is the e-mail I got from my division manager on January 29th, 2013: 'Subject: New Publication Review Committee (PRC) Procedures for C&A Science.'"

The email was reproduced in full and began, "This message is regarding the new Publication Review Committee procedures for C&A Science... "

The email noted that the new policy was to take effect on February 1, 2013. The anonymous scientist concluded, "You decide who's being untruthful."[16]

A few days after DFO tried to deny that there were any changes, the *Vancouver Sun* broke the story of a U.S. scientist, doing collaborative work with DFO, who refused to sign the new conditions. Calling it a "potential muzzle," Dr. Andreas Muenchow, of the University of Delaware, told the *Sun*, "I'm not signing it."[17] Muenchow had been working on a project with DFO scientists in the eastern Arctic since 2003.

In 2003, when the collaborative research project began, there were quite different rules about sharing data. The 2003 contract stated: "Data and any other project-related information shall be freely available to all Parties to this Agreement and may be used, disseminated or published, at any time."

Within days of the new publication policy, another DFO email was sent to scientists on February 7: now they must obtain consent before applying for research grants.

Clearly, the Harper administration was concerned that it was too difficult to muzzle scientists after their research was published. It was more effective to contractually control their research and data. The tightened control of science now began far earlier in the process. Stop the research from being submitted

124

to journals. Stop scientists from collaborating with others. Stop scientists from applying for research grants. Stop science from happening at all.

The elimination of whole branches of scientific work within the federal government, the slashing of governmental funds for science, and now a departmental veto on applying for research grants or submitting results to peer-reviewed journals are all part of an attempt to dismantle any governmental activities that could throw doubt on the wisdom of rapidly expanding fossil fuel exploitation.

Editorials condemning Canada's crackdown on science appeared in *Nature,* the *Economist,* and the *New York Times.* Yet Prime Minister Harper and PMO talking points continue to claim they are spending as much money on science as ever. And they likely are.

The 2012 budget stipulated that government grants in science were to be used for research that is "business-led and industry-relevant." Science grants are now disguised subsidies to Canadian corporations. Primary research, the kind of scientific inquiry that leads to new knowledge, will simply not be possible with those constraints. Building a better widget is our new goal. And that widget is likely being built for the oil sands.

Governments that understand science know that they need evidence before making decisions. Without science and research we don't know how much damage we are doing; we don't know if we are destroying our own nest. We are rendering ourselves ignorant just when we need knowledge to survive.

How is this possible? What drives a government to move from evidence-based decision making to decision-based evidence making?

Peter Timmerman is a professor of environmental studies at York University. Like visionary Ursula Franklin, he has a brilliant and original mind capable of shining a light on the ordinary and lighting up new meaning. He is also a friend. He makes me see words in new contexts; he once pointed out that we used to speak of public service and the common good, but now we generally only hear those words in the context of the Goods and Services Tax.

In a talk a few years ago, at a conference at the University of Toronto, he provided a key insight. It went (more or less) like this:

> We are convinced we are a secular society, but we are wrong.
>
> In fact, we only think we no longer have a state religion. We only think we have separated church and state, that we are a secular country.
>
> In reality, we have a state religion. It is complete with its own doctrine, catechism, set of rituals, liturgy, and priesthood. Our new religion is Econo-theism. We worship the economy.
>
> Nothing is allowed to offend the state religion. To question it is heresy. And its central organizing principle is selfish individualism—which all the great religions of the world teach us leads straight to doom.

And so Stephen Harper, in league with the dominant national religion of Econo-theism, must persecute any scientist whose work could compromise unfettered growth of fossil fuel production in Canada. Scientists are as dangerous to the new church as Galileo was to the old one. We have embraced ignorance.

This is the twenty-first-century equivalent of the Dark Ages. This is book burning and superstition run rampant. This is the administration of a steady, slow drip of poison to a weakening democracy.

Historical Manipulation of Science for Political Ends

126

Back in the 1930s, the Soviet ruler Josef Stalin had a problem with genetics; as a result, geneticists were branded traitors ("Trotskyite agents of international fascism"), stripped of their positions at government laboratories and universities, sent to prison, or even executed. Soviet biological sciences were hindered for more than a generation. The story of the Soviet geneticists has a distant resonance to the story of what is happening to government-sponsored environmental science in Canada today.

Genetics, the science of inheritance, was developed in the late 19th and early 20th century by scientists such as Gregor Mendel and T.H. Morgan, who did careful experiments demonstrating, among other things, the presence of dominant and recessive genes, as well as examining how genes combine to produce a variety of traits in animals and plants. Unfortunately, in Stalin's Soviet Union, there were a lot of things wrong with Mendelian genetics, including: Mendel was a Catholic priest (and thus stood against the atheistic Soviet regime), while Morgan was branded a capitalist (he was an American). Mendelian genetics didn't fit the Soviet ideology.

In the 1930s, Soviet genetics fell under the sway of Trofim Lysenko, an agronomist who proposed a different grounding for genetics. Lysenko's beliefs were that seed quality could be improved by challenging seeds with extremes of high humidity and low temperatures, and that these changes so produced would be inherited by the next generation of plants; indeed, he believed that new species of plants could be created through this process (much as the Soviet rulers believed that a new humanity could result from "challenge and struggle"). Instead of engaging in the necessarily long-term selection processes to produce the plant products that would be most valuable, Lysenko pushed Soviet plant science towards a method of crop improvement that led to crop failures and famine: genetic reality trumped Lysenkoist ideology.

The pursuit of scientific knowledge flourishes when scholars are free to pursue the best understandings they can come up with, knowing that others may come along afterwards and create more and better explanatory theories. Science can do what it does best when political systems encourage the freedom of exploration, and those systems are usually found in contexts of democratic governance.

Science, and scientists, do not always do well when states are run by rulers, especially rulers with strong authoritarian and ideological orientations that might be threatened by research findings. Rulers feel that they know what is right and what needs to be done in their domain, and see no need to compromise, to consult, to listen or to consider other opinions, all of which are essential elements of the toolkit of those who govern democratically. Rulers often see themselves as exceptional and exempt from the rules that they can impose on the ruled...

And now we have in Canada a situation where environmental scientists working for the government of Canada have been found to be doing research that is no longer in line with the ideology of our present rulers. Climate change scientists, eco-toxicologists, habitat specialists and more are not being lined up and shot as the geneticists were in Stalin's time, but they are seeing their positions eliminated, their funding and other resources constrained, and their ability to communicate restricted.

The ghost of Trofim Lysenko stalks Canadian government science. Science that produces results that fit with the Harperian science doctrine of "utility to corporations and industry above all else" seem to get the resources. Those government scientists engaging in the exploration of the major global issues of our time, but whose pursuits fall outside of Harperian ideology today are, either literally or metaphorically, being shown the door.[18]

RICHARD KOOL, ASSOCIATE PROFESSOR, SCHOOL OF ENVIRONMENT AND SUSTAINABILITY, ROYAL ROADS UNIVERSITY

Chapter Seven

HOW CANADA BECAME
A PETRO-STATE

THE FIRST SCIENTIST I knew who warned of runaway global warming was the visionary Dr. Digby McLaren. One of Canada's most respected scientists, he had been the head of the Geological Survey of Canada, and, when I met him, he was president of Canada's scientific academy, the Royal Society of Canada. He frequently met with me when I worked in McMillan's office as he pursued government support for a massive project, a scientific review of all aspects of global change. He was irreverent and witty and pulled no punches. He never agreed with me that we could find a path to sustainable development. He viewed any growth in human numbers and human influence as planetary Russian roulette.

He was also terribly entertaining. It was Digby McLaren, a vehement atheist, who pointed out to me that the fourth horseman of the Apocalypse in Revelations was a commodity trader. A set of scales (in some translations, a balance) is in his hands, and he's calling out spot trades: "A quart of wheat for a denarius, and three quarts of barley for a denarius; and what will I get for the oil and the wine?" (In some translations this is rendered as "Do not damage the oil and wine," and in others as "Give me a pipeline.")

It was Digby McLaren who threw me a lifeline when I was suddenly out of work after resigning over the Rafferty-Alameda dam permits (or damn permits). He gave me a job working on a part-time contract with the Royal Society.

When Digby first explained how human activity could launch positive feedback loops pushing the whole planet into uncontrollable levels of self-accelerating warming, I couldn't find any other scientists who were in agreement. I have to say I was vastly relieved that most climate scientists saw such a possibility as only hypothetical. Only decades of procrastination have led to the looming significance of the risk of runaway warming.

In a major 2013 paper, leading scientist and former head of the NASA Goddard Institute for Space Studies Dr. James Hansen and his co-authors concluded that "conceivable levels of human-made climate forcing could yield the low-end runaway greenhouse effect" based on inducing "out-of-control amplifying feedbacks such as ice sheet disintegration and melting of methane hydrates," through loss of permafrost.[1] The risk of human-induced climate change bringing about a runaway greenhouse effect is real. Even at the hypothetical "low-end" event identified by James Hansen, it is the kind of clear and present danger that requires political leadership. Instead, our political "leaders" continue to aid and abet disaster. As Hansen noted, "Governments are allowing and encouraging fossil fuel companies to go after every conceivable fuel which is an obtuse policy that ignores the implications for young people, future generations and nature. We could make substantial parts of the Earth uninhabitable."[2]

In 1972, the Club of Rome released its seminal report, *Limits to Growth*, on the threat of spiralling human numbers as we deplete resources and live beyond our means globally. *Limits to Growth* became a bestseller. I have my original copy, purchased when I was still in high school. I know I bought it a long time ago; it cost $2.75. As part of my activities in the school environment club, I bought every paperback I could and maintained a lending library for activists in one corner of the science lab where we tested the pH levels of various detergents.

The central tenets of *Limits to Growth* are well known. We are outstripping the carrying capacity of the planet. Population is growing exponentially. Resources are finite. Collapse will follow depletion of resources. It became understood that we would run out of non-renewable resources like fossil fuels. We had to conserve and properly manage renewable resources, such as fish and forests.[3]

Taking on the Club of Rome nearly a decade later, business economist Julian Simon argued that we would not run out of fossil fuels. In fact, he said that we would not run out of any resource, because, as a resource becomes scarce, the price goes up, creating an incentive to find more, to come up with technological innovations to access more of the resource, and ultimately to find substitutes.[4]

In many ways the two views—the Club of Rome versus Julian Simon (and his young telegenic acolyte, Bjorn Lomborg)—are perfect archetypes of the flawed economic-ecological debate.

In the short term, both views are correct. In the long term, only the Club of Rome analysis can be correct. As the 1970s bumper sticker put it, "Nature bats last."

Planetary life and processes are not static. We are part of an evolving universe, with natural cycles that have supported a healthy biosphere. But human activity is driving into reverse those natural systems. This is true of the carbon cycle, nitrogen cycle, and hydrological cycle, as well as species diversity; human activity has set in motion the largest extinction event since the dinosaurs. We are, against all odds, depleting the oceans and their renewable fisheries, along with renewable forests and soils, faster than we are destroying non-renewable fossil fuels.

Of course, as we run down the wild fishery, Bjorn Lomborg, in Simon-like fashion, celebrates that we are producing more fish through fish farms.[5] Left out of the debit sheet on their booming profitability is that coastal zones are being expropriated without compensation: from common property resources to privatized pollution pens. Meanwhile, the loss of those estuaries and coastal zones that once nurtured healthy ecosystems and spawning grounds for wild fisheries are simply not counted because we never put a price on them. It is not reflected in the GDP that the salmon grown in caged nets are being fed with fish that would otherwise be protein for communities in developing countries. Fish meal for carnivorous fish and the opportunity costs of that, the furtherance of ecological decline, is simply not on the ledger sheet. "All you can eat" Red Lobster shrimp comes at the price of sustainable communities along zones where the mangrove forests have been razed to make room for shrimp ponds. We only value what we measure. Externalities are not on the menu.

Ironically, we have actually expanded the supply of non-renewable fossil fuels. Global supplies of coal are so enormous that counting on coal scarcity to reduce greenhouse gases is a bet we can make on a dead planet. There is just too much coal to hope to run out within a time frame that matters to the atmosphere.

In the last decade or so, many have seized upon Hubbert's peak theory, named for M. King Hubbert, who argued that, because oil was finite, we would soon hit a point at which the newly discovered reserves of oil would fail to keep up with demand. This was described as hitting "peak oil" with economic dislocation as a result.[6] A whole movement, self-described "peakers" have warned that, any minute now, oil will simply be too expensive to buy and too scarce to find.

True, we have nearly run out of the easy-to-find, abundant oil and natural gas reserves. But, as Simon predicted, we are finding new sources of oil and natural gas. "Unconventional" oil and gas are being produced from shale (through hydraulic fracturing, known as "fracking") and, in other geological formations, from bitumen, scraped out of gaping canyons in open-pit mining or water injected "in situ" technology to force bitumen to the surface.

I remember sitting around the board room table of the

International Institute for Sustainable Development (IISD) in Winnipeg in 1996 when the CEO, my old friend David Runnalls, asked that IISD be given approval to enter into a contract with Shell to provide advice as production ramped up in the oil sands. Veteran climate scientist and fellow board member Jim Bruce shook his head sadly: "This is the worst news I could have heard." He described how unconventional oil from the Athabasca tar sands would drive up Canada's emissions of greenhouse gases.

The development of unconventional bitumen crude was the trump card to the Club of Rome. As we ran out of conventional fossil fuels, we found places to squeeze them out of the earth's crust elsewhere. Julian Simon was right.

Giving Simon credit for being more right than wrong is like giving the card shark credit for winning with marked cards. For years I have struggled with the irony that we are running out of renewable resources—fish and trees—and demonstrably not running out of fossil fuels. Beyond the irony, what accounts for such a perverse result?

It has only hit me recently: we don't measure the value of living things, so, as we wipe them out, we fail to notice. The last cod taken out of the draggers' nets off the coast of Newfoundland registered as a plus to the economy. Good news for GDP—right up to the moment it wasn't.

On the other hand, fossil fuels are priced as a result of market forces. Enormous corporate enterprises rely on maintaining reserves. We are not running out of oil and natural gas, and, in fact, global estimates of available reserves continue to show adequate supplies for the economy to remain plugged into fossil fuels into the next century. This fact allows us to live in denial. But it does not take into account the availability of the resource or the survival of human civilization. A more clear-eyed appraisal brings us back to agreeing with the Club of Rome. We have run out of room in the global atmosphere for the wastes from burning fossil fuels before we have run out of coal, oil, and gas.

133

To understand just how much less accessible the "unconventional" sources are than the "conventional" sources of oil and gas, it is instructive to check out something called EROEI (pronounced E-Roy), which stands for "energy returned on energy invested," or the ratio of how much energy it took to obtain the oil or gas in relation to the oil or gas we got.

When humans first started looking for oil, there were gushers. Think Jed Clampett of *The Beverly Hillbillies*: "Bubbling crude. Oil, that is. Black Gold, Texas tea." That kind of oil is essentially gone. The energy returned on energy invested in a historic 1901 gusher at Spindletop, Texas, was 100:1. In other words, you would get a hundred barrels of oil for an investment of one barrel. By the 1970s, the EROEI had dropped to 30:1—for every barrel of oil used to obtain the oil, 30 barrels are produced.[7] In less than a hundred years, the productivity had dropped by one-third. But consumers did not notice that decline.

Much more energy is required to obtain a barrel of oil from "unconventional" sources of oil and gas.

Bitumen is a molasses-like, viscous substance comprising about 10 per cent of all the background soil and rock in something we historically called the Athabasca tar sands. Such bitumen-laced soils exist in Saskatchewan, as well as other places around the globe, including current production in Venezuela. Tar sands have also been found in Madagascar, posing a threat to the sensitive and biologically rich environment.

The new public relations industry makeover has mysteriously decided that anyone who calls bitumen-rich soils "tar sands" is being disrespectful to Alberta. The politically correct term is "oil sands." I don't want to be disrespectful to anyone, so I call them oil sands. Given that bitumen is neither tar nor oil, I decided to use whatever term offends the fewest Albertans.

To get the bitumen separated from the soil is an energy-intensive and water-intensive process. Open-pit mining uses the largest heavy equipment anywhere in the world. On the surface, boreal forest, wetlands, and muskeg are removed, and the bitumen-laden earth is scraped out to depths of eighty metres. More than four hundred square miles of Alberta has undergone or is undergoing this deep, open-pit extraction of bitumen. It is one of the world's most extensive and damaging industrial projects.

If the bitumen is found deeper than eighty metres, the in situ method is used. In this process, warm water is injected down deep into the ground to pull the bitumen out through the well shafts. This method uses even more energy per barrel extracted and (not surprisingly) also uses more water.

When I toured the Suncor labs in Fort McMurray years ago, the cheerful woman scientist in a white lab coat explained, "Getting the bitumen is just like what we do in a washing machine: add warm water and stir."

Only bitumen requires a gargantuan washing machine using a lot of water. In fact, in 2011, the oil sands industry used an estimated 370 million cubic metres of water from the Athabasca River.[8] A lot of monster trucks haul the stuff, trucks that require the driver to climb the equivalent of two stories to reach the cab. That's a lot of hauling, digging, scraping, and heating water, and a serious amount of stirring.

The used water contaminated with a witch's brew of toxic compounds is held in tailings ponds. The "ponds" themselves are gigantic, estimated in 2013 to cover over 170 square kilometres of northern Alberta. The impoundments holding the water in place are some of the largest structures on earth. They have been inadequately monitored for decades, and the federal and provincial governments have agreed to a beefed-up "gold-plated monitoring system"—but only after Dr. David Schindler's research confirmed that pollution was leaching out of the tailings ponds and into the Athabasca River.

When we go back to the ratio of energy obtained versus energy invested, all the scraping, hauling, trucking, and processing to get at the bitumen leads to a drop in the EROEI to 7:1 for raw bitumen. By the time it is processed from bitumen into anything usable in an engine, the ratio is 3:1.[9]

As you can see, we are coming near the break-even point where it takes about as much oil to get a barrel of oil as you invest to get it. Cue the "law of diminishing returns." When is the Julian Simon contingent prepared to wave a white flag?

The most cost-effective barrel of oil to be found these days is the barrel of oil "found" by reducing inefficiencies in the way we waste oil in transportation, heating, lighting, and cooling. Years ago, Amory Lovins of the Rocky Mountain Institute coined the term "nega-watt" to refer to a unit of energy saved through energy efficiency, pointing out that it is just as valuable, at a far lower cost, as finding new supplies.[10] Demand-side management, finding oil through avoiding waste, has huge potential in a country like Canada where we waste more than half the energy we use.

Another problem is that the damage done by burning these previously uneconomical, inaccessible unconventional fossil fuel resources remains an externality. It remains external to what the market considers part of the equation—supply, demand, labour, and resources. Pollution remains "external."

The 1972 Club of Rome report discussed the hypothetical threat posed by massive increases in the warming gas carbon dioxide. At that time, global warming was a future threat. Now the chickens are coming home to roost. The evidence is all around us that ignoring the climate crisis threatens the lives of millions of people, coastal cities, food production, and ultimately the survival of human civilization. The worst-case scenarios for climate change are rarely discussed. The reality is that no one will know the end point for damage done by the climate crisis until we know when the transition from fossil fuels to renewable resources and greater energy productivity will take place.

If we had met the 1988 Toronto Conference challenge to reduce by 20 per cent below 1988 levels globally by 2005, or even the

Kyoto commitment to 6 per cent below 1990 by 2012, we would not be crossing dangerous thresholds in the atmosphere.

The current commitment, although not legally binding, on Canada and all the countries on earth is to avoid allowing the global average temperature to rise 2 degrees Celsius higher than it was before the Industrial Revolution. Stephen Harper personally committed to this in his brief appearance at the Copenhagen climate conference in 2009. To stay globally below 2 degrees, Harper promised Canada would reduce GHG to 17 per cent below 2005 levels by 2020. The latest Environment Canada figures confirm that by 2020, Canada will have made virtually zero progress to the target. But, according to the IPCC, even if all the voluntary targets taken on by industrialized countries at Copenhagen are met, the world's global average temperature will soar past 2 degrees, hitting 4 degrees by the end of the century, or even sooner.

Two degrees was identified by scientists as a level of global impact that would probably allow us to adapt to the changes we have now unleashed.

Two degrees sounds like nothing in a country where we can go from winter temperatures of 30 below zero to summers with 30 above, a swing of 60 degrees Celsius. Why worry about 2 degrees?

What is rarely explained—or, I fear, even understood—by Canadian politicians who claim to be committed to avoiding a rise of 2 degrees, is that global average temperature is a very big deal indeed. The difference in global averages between the temperature on earth now and ten thousand years ago, when most of Canada was under several kilometres of ice, was 5 degrees Celsius. In terms of average, 2 degrees is huge. Holding global average temperature below a rise of 2 degrees will not be easy, but it is essential. And to understand why it is essential, one needs to take account of a nasty little problem called "positive feedback loops."

Essentially, what is happening is that human-induced global warming is triggering processes that speed up the warming. For

137

example, when warmer ocean water because of human activity melts Arctic ice, a positive feedback loop is put in motion, with dangerous consequences.

The oceans are now becoming saturated with carbon. It used to be that the oceans acted as a "carbon sink," absorbing up to one-third of the carbon we put in the atmosphere. The ability of the oceans to absorb carbon has been weakened just when we need it most.

The ice itself performs an important function in regulating global climate. White ice bounces a good deal of solar radiation back away from the earth in a phenomenon called the albedo effect. As the ice melts, it reveals dark ocean water, which soaks up the heat of the sun, thus melting ice faster, to reveal more dark ocean water. A 2014 paper published in the Proceedings of the National Academy of Sciences puts the loss of Arctic ice at nearly thirty-five thousand square miles, on average, every year since 1979.[11] That's a lot more dark water, pulling in a lot more of the sun's energy—and heat.

The same dangerous speeding-up process occurs as forests burn as a result of drought conditions induced by global warming, releasing vast amounts of carbon as they burn, bringing on more warming. Frozen soils known as permafrost contain huge volumes of a potent greenhouse gas called methane. Although methane does not have as long a lifetime in the atmosphere as carbon, molecule for molecule, when it is present, it has twenty times the warming power of carbon. As the permafrost melts as a result of human activity, methane is released, speeding up the warming, to melt more permafrost.

At some point, there is a risk that human activity will push positive feedback loops into motion that will overtake our ability to reduce greenhouse gases enough to arrest the warming. This is often called "runaway global warming," in which 3 degrees becomes 4 and 4 degrees becomes 5 and so on. Although the chances that this will happen are somewhat remote, it is like

Russian roulette. We are leaving a loaded gun on the table for our children. We make the odds riskier with each passing year.

Two degrees isn't really a "safe" zone but represents a level of risk that most scientists believe will allow human societies to get through the multiple crises we are storing up for our children. Two degrees is likely too much warming to protect many low-lying island states from inundation. It is likely too high to protect summer ice over the North Pole. In fact, Hansen forcefully advocates that we hold warming to no more than 1 degree global average temperature rise. To the extent that scientists have proposed 2 degrees, the hope is that 2 degrees is not so high that we cannot put the brakes on warming and try to bring down atmospheric concentrations of carbon dioxide.

To avoid 2 degrees, we need to ensure that concentrations of carbon dioxide in the atmosphere stay below 425 parts per million (ppm).

Most scientists agree that we run the risk of exceeding 2 degrees with concentrations above 400 ppm. Based on readings of the chemistry of the atmosphere determined through those air bubbles in Antarctic ice cores, we know that carbon dioxide levels have not exceeded 280 ppm in well over one million years of the planet's history. In 2013, we crossed the 400 ppm threshold. As Ban Ki-moon told the Warsaw climate meeting, COP19, "We are the first humans in the history of Earth to breathe air with 400 ppm of carbon dioxide."

If we had a planetary health button on the dashboard of our cars, it would be flashing red.

The International Energy Agency (IEA), which tracks global supplies of fossil fuels, has not had an environmental focus, until recently. A few years ago, the IEA *World Energy Outlook Report* began calling for an end to government subsidies for fossil fuels, which amount to about $300 billion globally a year (compared with $30 billion a year for renewable energy). The conservative agency also began calling for a carbon tax, to encourage a

139

transition away from fossil fuels. The IEA reports started to warn the world that, although the supplies of fossil fuels were not running out, the atmospheric waste dump for pollution from burning those fuels was full. In fact, it was overflowing.

By 2012, the *World Energy Outlook Report* had become more specific. Given new, unconventional sources for oil and gas, the IEA warned that to avoid crossing the 2 degree mark, the world's governments would have to ensure that two-thirds of known reserves were untouched until 2050. Put another way, only one-third of known reserves of fossil fuels can be dug up and burned before 2050, if we want to avoid runaway global warming.

Reserves have expanded, but they must not be used.

Tragically, the Canadian government has ignored this central finding of the IEA. Conservative Party talking points use selective quotes from the same report to state that the world will continue to rely on fossil fuels for the foreseeable future. But there is a steadfast refusal by the prime minister and his cabinet to consider that we have to diversify our energy mix and use it more slowly to ensure that at least two-thirds of known reserves stay in the ground.

A European report building on the IEA policy advice has brought an economic lens to the IEA assertion that no more than one-third of known fossil fuel reserves can be burned before 2050. Because the book value of oil companies is premised on reserves that cannot be used, the oil industry assets are overvalued. This is called the "carbon bubble."

Stephen Harper is not listening to these warnings. He maintains a goal for oil sands production of six million barrels a day. In 2012, production was 1.8 million barrels, up from half a million barrels less than twenty years ago. It is astonishing that the prime minister wants to see production tripled when even the oil sands industry is not that ambitious. The Canadian Association of Petroleum Producers projects going to five million barrels a day.

The increasing obsession with boosting bitumen production is hobbling democracy and damaging Canada's international reputation. It also has changed our national characteristics. According to Alberta journalist Andrew Nikiforuk, that obsession is distorting us from a democracy to a "rogue petro-state."[12]

Canadian academic and internationally respected author Thomas Homer-Dixon agrees, writing in the *New York Times* that "Canada is beginning to exhibit the economic and political characteristics of a petro-state."[13]

The First Law of Petropolitics, as put forward by Thomas Friedman in the pages of the *Foreign Policy Review* in 2006, is that "the price of oil and the quality of freedom invariably travel in opposite directions."[14]

Petro-states have in common diminished democracy, low voter turnout, and greater centralization of power in ways that are unhealthy in a democracy. The lure of easy money, of living off oil rents, contributes to a loss of citizen engagement. Compounding the phenomenon of shrinking democracy is the increased ownership of the Canadian oil sands by state-owned enterprises (SOEs) of the People's Republic of China, in which no barrier exists between profits of SOEs and the Communist Party of China and the country's military. The largest behemoths of oil production are SOEs controlled by Beijing. PetroChina, Sinopec, and CNOOC (China National Offshore Oil Corporation) are heavily invested in Alberta's oil sands. China is now a capitalist country, proving that capitalism, democracy, and freedom do not inevitably coexist. Capitalism can be quite comfortable with despotic regimes. Democracies are a lot less predictable.

Not all oil-exporting nations drift toward petro-state status. The key policy difference between an oil-exporting democracy and a petro-state is whether the government decides to live off oil revenue. This is not a secret. In fact, former Alberta premier Peter Lougheed set out a plan for development of the oil sands, premised on managed and controlled growth, while setting aside oil rents in a heritage fund. He understood the risks of living off resource money. His successor, Ralph Klein, ripped up the

141

Lougheed plan and opted for unconstrained, unplanned development while allowing the government to operate on oil rents. He made the heritage fund a small piggy bank, squandering the chance to develop a significant fund, and went hog wild.

Lougheed's approach was followed in one smart jurisdiction: Norway. As a result, Norwegian democracy was not compromised and Norway's heritage fund is $900 billion (Canadian). Measured in Norwegian kroner, every citizen of Norway is a millionaire.[15] Meanwhile, Alberta is running deficits.

How could Canada's oil sands industry develop in such a reckless fashion, rejecting Lougheed's approach and pursuing what amounts to a drunken sailor's plan? The creation of an oil sands industry from the Athabasca tar sands is a story with the most improbable of beginnings. In the 1950s, Alberta was actually considering setting off an underground nuclear warhead to warm and lubricate the bitumen.[16]

The proposal got to a fairly advanced level before it occurred to one of the planners that selling radioactive bitumen would be a non-starter. The theoretical possibility of getting usable petroleum product out of bitumen remained just that—theoretical—until fairly recently.

Political support at all levels started long before Stephen Harper took the reins of the Alliance Party. The big boost to oil sands growth didn't come from Brian Mulroney; it came from Jean Chrétien.

No one in the environmental movement would have ever predicted that Chrétien's environmental record would make us nostalgic for Brian Mulroney. But that was what happened. In a vain attempt to shore up cabinet member and MP Anne McLellan's toehold for Liberals in Alberta, money was shovelled into the Athabasca tar sands (as they were then universally described) to boost production.

I can remember arguing with Jean Chrétien at a time when the prime minister was actually mixing with mere mortals at public events, something that no longer happens. I was frustrated by the lack of climate action from Chrétien's administration and told him so. He boasted of the many national parks he had created, going back to those he established in the Far North when he was minister responsible for parks, within the department of what was then energy, mines, and resources, under Prime Minister Trudeau. He rejected any notion that his environmental record was less than spectacular. "Those parks I created in the Arctic will be there forever!" I countered with "No, they won't. They are melting!"

Jean Chrétien was a key player in making a previously unattractive investment, the tar sands, into the major magnet for foreign investment that the "oil sands" are today.

In 1996, both Chrétien federally and Ralph Klein provincially created the sweetest set of fiscal conditions offered to fossil fuel investment anywhere on the planet—the world's lowest royalty rates and an accelerated capital cost (ACC) allowance that postponed any taxation until all capital investment was recouped. With oil selling at $30 a barrel, no large enterprise was going to make expensive investments in getting bitumen out of the ground. In 1996, bitumen production was less than a half million barrels a day. Federal ACCs would amount to approximately $2 billion a year over nearly two decades to help the fossil fuel sector grow. It was projected that by 2010, production would reach one million barrels of bitumen a day. In fact, the oil sands cruised past that target by 2000.

Whereas Peter Lougheed had anticipated ancillary developments such as upgraders and refineries that would enable the province to process bitumen into synthetic crude, the current regimes favour pushing the bitumen out of Canada as fast as possible to be processed elsewhere. Even as late as 2008, there were plans for more upgraders for Alberta. Those plans were 143 withdrawn as a result of the financial crisis, but even as the crisis receded and other projects came back on the drawing board, the upgraders did not. Instead of processing bitumen in Alberta into synthetic crude, suddenly there was a proposal to mix the bitumen with enough other fossil fuel by-products (known as diluents) to get them to flow into a pipeline and down to under-utilized refineries along the Gulf of Mexico or into tankers bound for refineries elsewhere. The Keystone XL pipeline is the replacement for the Alberta-based upgraders. Ancillary operations and investments make the Koch brothers the big winners if Keystone goes ahead.

According to a study by the International Forum on Globalization, David and Charles Koch stand to make $100 billion in Keystone profits. And when Keystone stalled, along came Enbridge pitching a twinned pipeline—one pipeline carrying diluents coming in on tankers from the Middle East, and the other heading back to the tanker port at Kitimat with the bitumen mixed with the diluents. That project is also all about shipping out raw product. None of these projects were being proposed when upgraders were in the queue.

The growth in the oil sands has distorted the Canadian economy. I had never heard of "Dutch disease" until June 2008, when I read the report on Canada released by the Organisation for Economic Co-operation and Development (OECD). The OECD is the rich boys' club within the community of nations. It is the think tank and data collector for the industrialized world.

I read the OECD report with great interest, astonished that this conservative body was calling on Canada to put in place a carbon tax. But it made this recommendation based not on an environmental analysis but on an economic one, as an antidote to the mild case of Dutch disease it saw taking hold in Canada.[17]

"Dutch disease" refers to the generic situation in which the currency of a country that discovers oil and starts exporting it rises in value and negatively affects those parts of the economy that benefitted from cheaper currency. The first place this was observed was the Netherlands, hence "Dutch disease." Netherland's oil exports from the North Sea raised the value of the guilder. As the Dutch guilder rose, the manufacturing sector suffered—with serious job losses. The OECD argued that Canada needed to be mindful of the threat of Dutch disease, especially because a higher Canadian dollar had already resulted in significant losses in the manufacturing sector and pulp and paper. In fact, even before the 2008 economic crisis hit, Canada had moved from budgetary surpluses to deficits, partly because the GST had been slashed and spending had increased but also because of job losses and the downturn in manufacturing and pulp and paper as the Canadian dollar rose in value.

I put it to Stephen Harper in the English 2008 leaders' debates that we were ignoring sound economic advice. By random seat selection, I was seated immediately to his left in the English-language debate. I asked if he had read the OECD report and its finding that Canada was suffering from Dutch disease. I could tell he wasn't expecting me to ask if he had read it. I also pointed out that he was supposed to have an economics background. Those debates had many intense moments, but Harper's look of surprise did nothing to reduce my interest in the skewing of our economy in the interests of promoting only one major export.

Running contrary to the petro-state narrative is the reality that, as a share of our GDP, energy sector revenues have declined since 1997. According to Statistics Canada, in 1997 the energy sector's contribution to Canada's GDP was 12 per cent. By 2013, it was down to 10 per cent. And that is the entire energy sector. The oil sands alone are closer to 3 per cent. And while the industry ads try to bedazzle us with the propaganda that the oil sands make it possible to run our hospitals and schools, less than 5 per cent of our taxes come from oil sands (4.3 per cent in 2011). In 2007, taxes paid by the oil and gas sector (larger than the oil sands alone) came to 8 per cent of taxable corporate income.[18] Although the slashing of corporate tax rates accounts for much of that precipitous drop, it is also related to the fact that our economy is still not all about bitumen.

145

The repeated exaggeration that our economy is somehow more dependent on the oil sands than other sectors seems to be convincing Canadians that these claims are true. It is also changing who we are.

As Andrew Nikiforuk noted, "Just as Margaret Thatcher funded her political makeover of Britain on revenue from North Sea oil, Harper intends to methodically rewire the entire Canadian experience with petrodollars sucked from the ground. In the process he has concentrated power in the prime minister's office and reoriented Canada's foreign priorities."[19]

Even the environmental movement plays into Big Carbon's hands when it exaggerates the economic lure of the oil sands. Economically, we have a lot of better choices. The myth of oil sands as the foundation for Canada's economic future is as false as the notion that we can ignore the consequences of the desperate mania for their exploitation.

More Money than Brains

The Canadian oil line to Toronto from Alberta goes through the American Midwest & the oil industry is completely controlled by U.S. companies.

FROM MY FATHER'S JOURNALS, NOVEMBER 11, 1973

The irony is that our overwhelming emphasis on money, our conviction that markets are the smartest systems of all, has resulted in three recessions and one global market meltdown in the past thirty years. The more-money-than-brains mindset has obvious disadvantages for brains, and the 2008 fiscal collapse suggests that it is not so great for money either. But this crash also gives North Americans a chance to reassess our values and reconsider what we want from our political institutions, education systems, and markets...

The more-money-than-brains mindset confuses two things. It treats money as an end in itself and knowledge as a mere means to an end. When we treat money this way, we sanction the kind of excesses that crashed the stock markets and damaged the economy. We encourage students to mistake low cunning and greed for intellect and skill. When we treat knowledge as mere means to an end, we create contraptions without regard for the consequences.

LAURA PENNY, *More Money than Brains*[20]

Chapter Eight

ENGAGING THE PROFIT MOTIVE TO FIGHT CLIMATE CHANGE

ONE OF MY dearest friends lives on Salt Spring Island. In 2003, when my mother died, Dorothy Cutting offered to be my adopted mom. I snapped up the offer. We have a lot in common, even if she has a couple of decades on me. We both grew up in the U.S. and even attended the same high school, and Dorothy is also a climate activist.

We met because she contacted the Sierra Club of Canada office in 2002, deeply affected by the book 2030: Confronting Thermageddon in Our Lifetime by Bob Hunter, another dear friend who left us too soon. In the book, Bob, a founder of Greenpeace, tells a compelling personal story of awakening to the reality of climate change and recounts some of what I have said in this book: we are in serious trouble, and if we do not rise to the challenge and fix the problems, our children will be in grave danger—danger not of their making.

When Dorothy phoned my Sierra Club office, she had one simple question: Would it help to give a copy of 2030 to every member of parliament? And, she added, if it would help, she was prepared to buy the books. Andrew Dumbrille, the young man who took her call, came to me about it. "She sounds like a really nice grandmother and she sounds serious."

It wasn't every day we got a call like that. Our climate campaigner, John Bennett, called her back and suggested she fly to Ottawa and personally present the book to Canada's minister of the environment. Back then, we had an environment minister who actually cared about the environment, Victoria MP David Anderson. She recoiled. "With what I have learned about greenhouse gas emissions," she said, "I would never fly to Ottawa!"

It was the beginning of an amazing journey as Dorothy bought a hybrid car and drove across the country. She had never done this before, but she rejected our suggestion we get her a co-pilot. The only company she wanted was her dog. And she firmly refused to have a fixed itinerary of any kind. Every day Andrew would get a call from Dorothy and run to my office. "Who do you know in Red Deer? She thinks that's where she'll be tonight."

Fortunately, I tend to know at least a few people everywhere, and that would give us a starting point for answering these frantic phone calls. We would locate friendly billets, happy to take a climate activist grandmother and her dog, and we would line up media interviews for her. She had the car tailored with a message across the bumper: "I'm driving my hybrid car to give my grandchildren a future."

We have worked together ever since—to get Canada to ratify Kyoto, which happened the following year and, much later, to see a real climate plan put in place. And now I am both her adopted daughter and her member of parliament.

Today, as Canada fails the world and as our greenhouse gases rise, I find we can talk less and less about the challenge. Dorothy no longer believes in trying to make global instruments like Kyoto work. The only way I can see to move societies fast enough to a low-carbon economy is through a shared, global, binding legal commitment. "We just don't see things the same way," she says.

Still, she has not given up hope. She draws strength from what she ascribes to a shared survival instinct, working in concert with our supreme innate intelligence.

On one thing we agree: the worst is unthinkable.

As German Green Party founder Petra Kelly, whom I also had the privilege to know, once said, "We, the generation that faces the next century, can add the solemn injunction: 'If we don't do the impossible, we shall be faced with the unthinkable.'"[1]

Telling me it is impossible to avoid runaway global warming does not make me believe it is inevitable that humanity will fail to rise to the challenge. We will, because we must.

Remaining hopeful in the face of increasingly dispiriting evidence is a matter of moral courage. All the uncertainties in climate science seem to resolve toward the threat being worse than predicted. And not everything in a complex area of science like global atmospheric chemistry is predictable.

We keep experiencing "nasty shocks." The 1980s models did not anticipate coral reef bleaching (at relatively low levels of ocean temperature change) or ocean acidification as carbon in the air mixes into ocean surface layers, creating carbonic acid to melt shells in sea creatures. This threat to our oceans remains whether or not any nation ever approves some crazed geo-engineering scheme to add particulates to the upper atmosphere to create cooling to offset the warming. The carbon dioxide content of the atmosphere is mixing with ocean water and threatening the life of our oceans.

We didn't know that the jet stream's stability in moving rapidly and horizontally at mid-latitudes would be weakened to such an extent that it would start moving slowly in lazy loops that leave high pressure zones sitting on some areas, while low pressure zones sit on others. Scientists at Rutgers University have linked the warming Arctic to the changed patterns of the jet stream, helping to explain extreme events like Superstorm Sandy and the extreme and persistent weather that floods one part of the world while driving extreme heat—or extreme cold—in others.

Being hopeful is not the same thing as being unrealistic. This is not the dewy-eyed dreamy hope of the deluded. In the context of the climate crisis, hope is hard work. As David Orr, environmental studies professor at Oberlin College, put it, "Hope is a verb with its sleeves rolled up."[2]

This is where I ask you to have hope. And work to make it viable.

Fortunately, in this we are not alone. We have strong and unlikely allies. We have entrepreneurs, inventors, and a whole cadre of new green, clean-tech advocates. We have an industrial revolution of a new kind.

People in the middle of a revolution are often the last to know. When large, complex systems lose equilibrium, those least likely to notice are in the middle. Often they think they still hold the levers that control the situation. Like Nicolae Ceausescu in Romania, bussing in eighty thousand supporters to fill the plaza in front of parliament, but unaware that his total control was about to be blown away by the laughter of young people. In his televised address to the nation, from the balcony of the building, viewers across the country saw him flinch when from the fringes of the rally came the sound of young people laughing at him.

Similarly, those in the Kremlin were among the last to know the USSR was collapsing. In disequilibrium, we may assume we are about to right ourselves, when, in fact, we are about to make a complete change.

Not all revolutions are about deposing dictators. I remember the first time I heard someone in the media say, "Someday every home will have a computer." And I looked at the picture of a big ugly hunk of metal taking up an entire room. Why would we want a computer in every home? What on earth would it do? And if we wanted one, who would be able to afford it?

Now most homes have several computers. There are desktops and laptops and gizmos and gadgets that are more about entertainment than work and computation. I never imagined that a computer and the internet would be able to replace television networks. Neither did the television networks. Some homes are run by computers with "smart" devices. Computers now can fit in your pocket and under the hood of your car. They are ubiquitous.

It will be like that with renewable energy and clean tech,, which are getting better and better, but the noise is still all about coal, oil, and natural gas. In our fraught state of addiction, we are fracking and scraping the stuff at the bottom of the petroleum barrel. The dinosaur fuels get all the attention, but their day is done. As Sheik Yamani said in 1973 in the first oil shock, "The Stone Age did not end because we ran out of stones, but because we found something better."[3]

Our problem is that not all the fossils are in the fuels.

Smarter options are within reach.

In 2012, investment in clean tech and renewables was nearly equal to investment in fossil fuels. According to the IEA, the amount of government subsidies to fossil fuels is ten times larger than subsidies to renewable energy. Governments are in the way, continuing to invest taxpayers' funds in subsidizing the wrong energy choices. The wealthiest corporations on earth are still on the dole to dig up fossil fuels. As Massachusetts congressman Ed Markey put it, "Subsidizing an oil company to find oil is like subsidizing a fish to swim ... "[4]

The technologies to reduce fossil fuel dependency have been around for a long time. At the time of the oil shock in the early 1970s, there was a burst of interest in fuel-efficient cars and in shifting to wind and solar. The large oil companies bought up the best patents on green energy and kept the pedal to the metal. Henry Kissinger lamented in a post-Kyoto interview that, had the U.S. stuck with plans in the works in the 1970s, it would now be completely independent of foreign oil imports.

The renewable energy options continue to diversify. The price keeps coming down. We have fuel cells that run city buses in 153 Chicago on hydrogen, with nothing but water vapour coming out the tailpipe. Those fuel cells are homegrown Canadian technology from Ballard Power Systems of Vancouver. According to

Amory Lovins, fuel cells work even better for heating and cooling buildings, and cars running on them could plug into the building, selling energy to the building owner and making money for the employees through power generation, while they are busy at their desks and production lines.

Hydrogen is a means of conveying energy rather than a source of energy itself. It can be made by wind power, hydro power, nuclear power, or coal. So it is important to know the source of the hydrogen when calculating its carbon footprint. But its potential as a way of delivering reliable power generation from clean energy sources is enormous.

Similarly, "Blue Fuel," pioneered by Juergen Puetter, CEO of Sidney, BC-based Aeolis Wind, can be derived from wind energy. While promoting and building large-scale wind projects in northern BC, Puetter realized the wind energy potential outstripped current demand. The available wind energy can be cost-effectively stored by making low-carbon liquid transportation fuels. Fuels such as methanol can be readily transported by rail or truck and are not dependent on building new pipelines. The first large-scale facility is now in the permitting process and slated for operation by 2018.

Traditionally, the downside of renewable energy is that it is peak load and not base load. Base load is that kind of power that comes from coal, oil, or nuclear power plants. Renewable energy is described as peak load. If the wind isn't blowing or the sun isn't shining, you have a gap in production. But once that small gap is bridged, through some form of storage, renewables will be able to completely replace fossil fuels.

Storing renewable energy is as simple as using wind power to pump water up into a reservoir, to release later when the wind isn't blowing or the sun isn't shining. It is a simple and elegant marriage of wind or solar with renewable hydroelectricity. The Nordic countries have already figured it out. Denmark's wind-generated electricity is shared across the grid with Norway. When the wind is blowing, its energy pumps water into reservoirs in

154

Norway. When the wind isn't blowing, Norway opens the sluices to drive hydro power. Peak to base in one elegant solution.

The Netherlands has been supporting research into storing wind energy as compressed air. Other countries have focussed on converting wind to hydrogen, as a pilot project in Prince Edward Island once did. Former U.S. secretary of energy Steven Chu, who is also a Nobel Laureate in physics, spoke at the climate meetings in Copenhagen about one of his "long-shot" investments—a new generation of batteries. He pointed out that no significant new research in batteries had been conducted for years, but that a swimming pool–sized magnesium battery could, in theory, power a whole city.

Once we solve the glitch in storage systems for renewables, there will be nothing to prevent combinations of green and clean energy sources from taking over from fossil fuels. Especially once green power becomes cheaper than fossil fuels.

The price for photovoltaics, which directly convert sunlight to electricity, is coming down. Other new developments in renewable energy are reported nearly daily. Spinning photovoltaics, like small flowers, could produce cheap electricity to power urban buildings. Vats of algae could be used to make biofuels for vehicles, as opposed to the unsustainable idea of diverting food crops like corn to ethanol. Low-flow tidal technology is being used to capture the moon's impact on our coastal zones. Many of these innovations are commercialized. Many are Canadian. But few are commercialized in Canada. We are asleep at the clean-tech switch.

Large multinationals are paying attention. DuPont, which invented alternatives to its ozone-depleting chlorofluorocarbons, made another quantum leap in relation to climate by pledging to cut its carbon emissions by 65 per cent below 1990 levels by 2010. The company didn't hit that target; it sailed past it. By 2007, emissions were 80 per cent below 1990 levels, and the company made a profit of $2.2 billion. While some companies insist that cutting carbon reduces profits, DuPont has proven the opposite. Waste is not good for profits.

DuPont's experience is not unique. Major global corporations—including Johnson & Johnson, 3-M, Walmart, and Toyota—have balance sheets that prove that reducing carbon helps the bottom line.

One of the most visionary of industry leaders was the late Ray Anderson. This gentle Georgian with a lilting southern accent and a profound faith came to embracing corporate sustainability when he was already CEO and founder of Interface, the largest commercial floor covering company in the U.S. I heard him tell this story many times over the years I had the joy of knowing him.

His road to Damascus conversion occurred when he was challenged to give a speech on sustainability. Not knowing much about it, he opened a book by another trailblazer in corporate responsibility, Paul Hawken. Hawken, who made his fortune in the natural foods business, recognized the inherent unsustainability of the corporate growth model. As founder and CEO of Erewhon, he took the concept of natural foods from fringe outlets to a major and successful national food distributor. His book *The Ecology of Commerce* set out his central dilemma: no matter how conscientious his company was, the reality of all human industrial activity is that we are killing the planet. With the insights of an entrepreneur, he wrote that he knew industrialists did not wake up in the morning wondering what they could do to destroy the planet that day. We have, he wrote in understated fashion, "a design problem."

This was the book Ray Anderson had picked up to prepare a speech on something called "sustainability." Ray would describe reading it as being like a "spear in the chest." He woke to some terrible realities. I remember him describing what we were doing to the biosphere as being "a steady march to the grave."

156 Ray Anderson made Interface an exemplar of sustainability in business. He described it as the challenge of climbing Mount Sustainability, setting the corporate goal as zero waste. He reduced pollution enough to shut down smokestacks and pipes dumping

waste water. Interface funded electrical generation by capturing methane from the local landfill. Not only was it sufficient for the company's own energy needs; it powered the town, dramatically reducing greenhouse gases.

In Canada, Interface relied on solar energy for its plant. The material in the carpets changed from toxic to positively wholesome. Not only was their used carpet compostable, you could eat it—but Ray usually added, "You wouldn't want to." And the concept of their business model changed from selling floor covering to leasing a service. Once the service provided by the floor covering was completed, the carpet could go back to the manufacturer. The floor covering came in tiles so that carpeting in busy traffic areas in an office could be replaced easily—without stripping out an entire floor covering and sending it to the landfill. Anderson's innovations had the effect of exciting and motivating his team. Employee satisfaction soared. And, even now, after his death, the corporate philosophy has remained intact. Employees are still committed to Mission Zero.

Canada has its homegrown examples of companies that have exceeded targets, reduced pollution, and generated higher profits as a result. Robert Schad, German immigrant to Canada and tireless innovator, built Husky Injection Molding Systems from scratch. He also drove the company to cut its CFCs and greenhouse gases by reducing waste of water and energy.

So if you can make money by reducing pollution, why do we still have pollution? We are back to Hawken's observation: we have a design problem. We keep subsidizing waste and pollution. We make it difficult to invest in the technologies that reduce waste. Upfront capital costs are hard to justify, even if they reduce future costs.

If we were serious about innovation in Canada, if we wanted to ensure that our economy stayed vibrant, the last thing we would do is focus on drilling the oil sands and fracking natural gas. We would diversify, encourage innovators, and ensure that policies aid the commercialization of smart new technology. We would build supply chains and a flourishing intersection of supply chains for local consumption and export. We would, in other words, develop policies most favourable to small and medium-sized enterprises. We would, as the Pembina Institute research demonstrates is possible, build the Canadian clean-tech sector from its current $9 billion market share to $60 billion by 2020.[5]

The problem is not that governments are not doing enough to fight global warming. It's that governments, particularly the Harper administration, are actually in the way.

If we were serious about reducing greenhouse gases, we would have a national strategy developed through consultation and negotiations with all other jurisdictions. We would set ambitious targets. The number one goal should be to shut down coal-fired electricity generation. The coal plants in Alberta alone still produce more carbon pollution than the oil sands (although if oil sands development expands, it will eclipse coal soon). Of the Canadian provinces, only Ontario has shut down its coal-fired electricity. In addition to Alberta and Ontario, electricity in Saskatchewan, New Brunswick, Nova Scotia, and Newfoundland and Labrador is still based on fossil fuel. In much of the Territories, expensive imported diesel is the source of power.

As a transitional source of electricity, coal-fired plants can be retrofitted to natural gas or even biomass. But the goal should be to transition to renewable energy.

In 2002, the Climate Action Network (CAN) and the David Suzuki Foundation engaged Canadian energy analyst Ralph Torrie to conduct a major study of Canada's energy grid. As executive director of Sierra Club and a member of the CAN executive, I was excited by the solutions contained in Torrie's report. It was a real eye-opener. Torrie demonstrated that improvements in energy productivity (in other words, reducing the amount of energy we waste) since 1970 had "created" more energy than all new oil, coal, nuclear, and gas energy combined over the same period:

With almost no government assistance, in the absence of well organized institutional and financial infrastructure for its delivery, and against a heavily subsidized and highly organized competition from oil, gas and nuclear power, the demand side has still managed to outperform the supply side of the energy economy since 1970.

The question arises: How much more could we get from this resource if we *tried*? [6]

Just as in the postwar era, with economies thriving through improvements in labour productivity, now we need to make quantum leaps in energy productivity. By Torrie's calculations, using existing technologies, we could have met and exceeded Kyoto targets, without having to install any new power-generating plants, while shutting down all coal plants and nuclear reactors. The only new piece we needed was interconnectivity east–west in our electricity grid. We invited Natural Resources Canada and anyone in the fossil fuel lobby to find any flaws with the study. No one did.

Clearly, our problem is less how we generate power and more how much we waste. Because Canadians waste more than half the energy we use, plugging those leaks in the system will yield better results. We will gain more cuts to carbon at the lowest cost per ton while creating jobs across the country and improving our quality of life. At the same time, we will reduce the carrying costs of our residential, commercial, and institutional buildings. Energy efficiency wins hands-down as the win-win-win first step.

To get there, governments need to stop subsidizing dirty energy and eliminate those bogus economic signals that distort the marketplace. Subsidies to fossil fuels and the failure to put a price on carbon distort the market. Simply put, we have to price pollution so that we drive those pesky "externalities" into our economic models.

We also must avoid the techno-optimism that assumes the transition will be easy. As Canadian environmental economist and modeller Mark Jaccard warns, there will be winners and losers in the economy. Sorting out the fairest way to rapidly reduce emissions is part of any set of policy prescriptions allowing renewable energy and energy efficiency to be winners. Jaccard writes:

> At the federal level in Canada, a key issue will be to make sure that national climate policy is not seen as unfair to any particular region. This is not easy, in part because of different perceptions of fairness and in part because some regions are more GHG-intensive and therefore may be expected to incur greater costs in the process of reducing emissions.[7]

We are running out of time to implement economically profitable solutions. The more we procrastinate and delay, the greater the likelihood that drastic reductions in carbon will be dislocating in the economy. If we fail to act when a soft landing is possible, our future choices will be far more disruptive. When it's too late for a carbon tax, we may have no choice other than allocating a personal carbon ration. That is just one more reason delay is not an option.

While the price drops for green energy and clean tech, we are in a race against time. Government action, especially in Canada, is impeding progress, while entrepreneurs and innovators of all kinds are racing to the rescue. They will do well by doing good.

Our job is to move government from the problem side of the ledger to the solution side.

"Sacrifice Is for Suckers" and Other Mantras of the 1 Per Cent

ON OCTOBER 16, 2001, I was in Brainerd, Minnesota, to speak at a conference of the Environmental Grantmakers Association, foundations that provide charitable grants for environmental work. The keynote was delivered by a very emotional Bill Moyers. His speech arced through the pain of loss, of friends caught in the

9/11 attack, and of the courage of the firefighters, police officers, and public health workers. It was a brilliant evisceration of the politics of self-interest. Here is an excerpt from that speech:

> While in New York, we are still attending memorial services for firemen and police, while everywhere Americans' cheeks are still stained with tears. While the President calls for patriotism, prayers and piety, the predators of Washington are up to their old tricks in the pursuit of private plunder at public expense. In the wake of this awful tragedy wrought by terrorism, they are cashing in.
>
> Would you like to know the memorial they would offer the almost six thousand people who died in the attacks? Or the legacy they would provide the ten thousand children who lost a parent in the horror? How do they propose to fight the long and costly war on terrorism America must now undertake?
>
> Why, restore the three-martini lunch—that will surely strike fear in the heart of Osama bin Laden. You think I'm kidding, but bringing back the deductible lunch is one of the proposals on the table in Washington right now. There are members of Congress who believe you should sacrifice in this time of crisis by paying for lobbyists' long lunches. And cut capital gains for the wealthy, naturally—that's America's patriotic duty, too. And while we're at it, don't forget to eliminate the Corporate Alternative Minimum Tax, enacted fifteen years ago to prevent corporations from taking so many credits and deductions that they owed little if any taxes. But don't just repeal their minimum tax; give those corporations a refund for all the minimum tax they have ever been assessed.
>
> You look incredulous. But, that's taking place in Washington, even as we meet here in Brainerd this morning. What else can America do to strike at the terrorists? Why, slip in a special tax break for poor General Electric, and slip inside the Environmental Protection Agency while everyone's distracted, and torpedo the recent order to clean the Hudson River of PCBs. Don't worry

about NBC, CNBC, or MSNBC reporting it; they're all in the GE family.

It's time for Churchillian courage, we're told. So how would this crowd assure that future generations will look back and say, "This was their finest hour?" That's easy. Give those coal producers freedom to pollute. And shovel generous tax breaks to those giant energy companies; and open the Alaskan wilderness to drilling—that's something to remember the 11th of September for. And, while the red, white and blue waves at half-mast over the land of the free and the home of the brave—why, give the President the power to discard democratic debate and the rule of law concerning controversial trade agreements, and set up secret tribunals to run roughshod over local communities trying to protect their environment and their health. It's happening as we meet. It's happening right now.

If I sound a little bitter about this, I am. The President rightly appeals every day for sacrifice, but *to these mercenaries sacrifice is for suckers.* So I am bitter, yes, and sad. Our business and political class owes us better than this. After all, it was they who declared class war twenty years ago and it was they who won. They're on top. If ever they were going to put patriotism over profits, if ever they were going to practice the magnanimity of winners, this was the moment. To hide now behind the flag while ripping off a country in crisis fatally—fatally!—separates them from the common course of American life. Some things just don't change . . .

Mencken got it right—the journalist H.L. Mencken, who said that when you hear some men talk about their love of country, it's a sign they expect to be paid for it." [8] (emphasis added)

Chapter Nine

RESCUING DEMOCRACY
FROM POLITICS

BEFORE QUITTING SIERRA CLUB to run for leader of the Green Party, I had a vague sense that partisan politics would be unpleasant. Making the transition from the world of non-governmental political engagement was, as I have confessed, driven by my concern that Stephen Harper would dismantle our environmental policies. I had ample reason to view excessive partisanship as a threat to Canada.

In the midst of the 2006 election campaign, while I was cooking dinner at home, I received a telemarketing call on behalf of the NDP. I knew the NDP used a marketing company called Stratcom, and I knew I was speaking with a paid telemarketer working from a script.

He told me now was the time to increase my support for the NDP. I said, "I am not very happy with the NDP right now. All of your ads are about the Liberal sponsorship scandal. There is no mention of what Harper would do to our climate policy."

"You should not be worried," said the Stratcom script reader, moving to the "how to handle Harper-phobic voter" part of the pre-approved party line. "The most Harper can get will be a minority and with Jack Layton and a strong NDP team, Harper will not be able to do anything."

I said words to the effect of, "Are you crazy? Even with a minority, don't you know how our system works? He can cancel Kyoto. Cancel our climate plan and do all this without a single vote in the House of Commons."

What I found most disturbing about the telemarketer was that the script written for people like me, who were angry about the NDP electoral strategy, would lead to a Conservative win. Partisanship was trumping common sense.

I knew that even a minority government under the Harper Conservatives would be very bad news, but the litany of acts of vandalism against parliamentary democracy has been more devastating than I had imagined.

Since 2006, we have had a prime minister who has shut down Parliament to avoid political embarrassment (something virtually unheard of throughout the Commonwealth nations) and twice done so illegitimately; a prime minister who has placed his executive powers above the law by refusing to accept the supremacy of Parliament. He has ignored inconvenient court rulings and even impugned the reputation of the chief justice of the Supreme Court of Canada. He has also gagged researchers and scientists and suppressed scientific information, and he has forced through massive omnibus laws without adequate care or review, in the process making drastic transformational changes to laws and policies—from taxing income trusts to changing the retirement age for Canadians, to overhauling our criminal justice system, and to cancelling decades' worth of environmental laws.

None of these actions were proclaimed in campaign platforms. In fact, on income trusts and retirement age, the opposite was pledged. Had Harper promised to cut scientific research and shut down libraries and repeal environmental laws to grease the gears for pipelines and tankers, he could never have formed government at all.

The same prime minister, for the first time in Canadian history, has treated our international treaty obligations like old leaves to be burned in fall bonfires.

The Harper administration has been disrespectful to the UN and in the process has alienated many of our traditional admirers and supporters. One incident that is burned into my memory was Stephen Harper's reaction to the killing of a Canadian peacekeeper at a UN observer post in southern Lebanon. It was August 2006, and the Israeli assault of Lebanon followed the Hezbollah shelling of Israel from locations within Lebanon. An Israeli bomb hit the UN observer station, killing a member of Princess Patricia's Light Infantry, Major Paeta Hess-von Kruedener. Right up to the moment their station was hit, the UN peacekeepers had been in radio contact with the Israeli army, confirming their location and asking for the shelling to stop. Nationals from Finland, China, and Austria were also killed. Their governments condemned the shelling, calling Israel's actions unacceptable, but our prime minister attacked the United Nations. "We want to find out why this United Nations post was attacked and also why it remained manned during what is now, more or less, a war, during obvious danger to these individuals," said Stephen Harper.[1]

Canada was the only nation to drop out of the United Nations Convention to Combat Desertification (UNCCD). In defending this move, Foreign Affairs Minister John Baird criticized the UNCCD as a "talk fest."[2] Prime Minister Harper dismissed the convention as a bureaucratic waste, suggesting that the $350,000 that Canada contributes was "not an effective way to spend taxpayers' money."[3]

This is ironic, given that this amount is a fraction of the sums the Conservative government routinely spends on ads supporting its own economic platforms, largely for programs that are being reannounced, not yet or never funded. One single government ad for the Keystone pipeline in the *New Yorker* cost over $200,000.[4] Forgetting for the moment that the UNCCD represents a significant scientific initiative aimed at the causes of one of Africa's (and increasingly the rest of the world's, including Canada's) leading agricultural problems, clearly Stephen Harper

165

does not understand the principles of compromise and leverage in international affairs. These were principles applied in Canada diplomacy, and as a result, Canada has been looked to for leadership internationally. International leadership came at a low cost to the taxpayer, such as the small cost of staying in the UNCCD. Such multilateral efforts have paid enormous dividends to Canadian business and Canadian tourists abroad.

Canadian diplomats always had a reputation for being among the best and brightest of international negotiators—until now, when, muzzled by a PMO anxious that all keep on message, and directed by a prime minister who seems to think he can do it alone, we are losing both our global reputation and our effectiveness in our international dealings.

As Harrison Samphir of the University of Winnipeg noted in *Rabble.ca,* "Including its withdrawal from the Kyoto Protocol in 2011, Canada has repeatedly shunned international scientific cooperation while committing itself to the ideological dispersal of aid funds. The role-reversal of NGOs—from 'idealism to imperialism,' as one text calls it—is a key mechanism of this reinvented 'humanitarianism' (remember Canada's desertion of KAIROS, the non-profit which assisted Palestinian refugees and children in other starving nations?)."[5]

But the problem is larger than just a prime minister who seems bent on reinventing Canadian democracy to conform to some personal and yet-to-be publicly acknowledged libertarian ideology. It is about how his actions are reshaping the economy in ways that will not benefit Canadians either fairly or evenly. It is about how the Canadian economy is being reshaped in ways that largely benefit the interests of a few large foreign corporations while ignoring the dangers of an increasingly unviable, fossil fuel–based economy. There are opportunity costs in putting all our eggs in the bitumen basket. Manufacturing, pulp and paper, and tourism have all suffered in recent years. Innovation is lagging. We are losing the potential benefits to all Canadians in quality of life, jobs, economic prospects, and a safer, better world for our children offered by a renewable and sustainable economy.

Where there should be outrage, all too often, there seems to be a collective yawn. Joseph de Maistre, the nineteenth-century political philosopher, once observed, "Every country has the government it deserves."[6] But is this what Canadians either deserve or want?

Canadians have allowed what is essentially an elected dictatorship to reverse decades of policies that were drawn from the well of political consensus. As Joe Clark recounted in *How We Lead*, Commonwealth leaders were surprised that his policies were so close to Trudeau's. He explained that the policies were not Liberal or Progressive Conservative; they were Canadian.[7] Left, right, or centre, previous governments cared about environmental protection. Left, right, or centre, previous governments cared about our international reputation. Left, right, or centre, previous governments respected parliamentary traditions, civil liberties, trade union rights. And left, right, or centre, previous governments formed policy based on at least some degree of collective approval.

How is it that with the benefits of democracy, the right to speak freely and gather in the town square to protest governmental actions, and the ability to organize, lobby, and press for policies that will achieve the highest values for the common good, we privileged Canadians are so disengaged?

We need to be deeply concerned about why Canadians, among the most freedom-loving of people, are turning off politics and losing our rights, privileges, and patrimony to special interests.

Engagement requires a degree of trust and respect in political institutions. But being cynical about government is now firmly entrenched in our political culture. The behaviour of our politicians is fodder for satire, in many cases deservedly so. Sadly, polls show that politicians are less respected or admired than those in most other professions.

However, the reality is that members of parliament, virtually without exception, are hard-working and decent. I count most of them as friends. If they were given the freedom to speak from their own perspectives, on behalf of their constituents, the House of Commons would not be the toxic soup of vituperative commentary that it is today. Those attacks and the feigned contempt for members of another party are required of MPs by the backroom spin doctors of their parties. Conservative MPs have come over to me, after reading from a script that attacked me, to say they are sorry. Once one Conservative MP came to apologize because his wife happened to see his low-blow attack on CPAC (the Cable Public Affairs Channel that broadcasts Parliament) and insisted that he do so.

Parliament is not a bad place because of the members of parliament. It is a bad place because the large political parties have executed a complete takeover of MPs' freedom of action and freedom of speech. Many Canadians see this in relation to the Conservatives, but the NDP and the Liberal caucuses are also on a short leash. In fact, under Thomas Mulcair, the NDP has a record of 100 per cent party discipline. No New Democrat MP has strayed from the voting instructions on any vote. The same cannot be said of the Conservatives.

Part of the blame surely also rests on the current practice of politics: the culture of attack ads as substitute for fair-minded debate; smear campaigns as substitute for reasoned assessment of experience, character, and ability; voter suppression through robo-calls, as in the 2011 election where thousands of voters received calls intended to misdirect them from the correct polling place; a government in constant election mode, with an imperious disregard for Parliament, and a rigidly partisan and uncompromising party discipline that stifles MPs' consciences and very often the interests and desires of their own constituents.

168

To watch Question Period on television is enough to make most people change the channel. I see school groups come into the House only to have teachers shepherd their young charges out of the chamber as MPs descend into behaviour no teacher would allow in a classroom. We rail against bullying, only to see the swagger of bullies, the taunts of classroom bad boys, in the House of Commons.

We have a prime minister who has introduced the most vicious use of attack ads, aimed at destroying the public perceptions of the personalities of his opponents. For the first time in our history, the airwaves are polluted with hyper-partisan attack ads months—and even years—before an election.

This climate has clearly alienated many voters.

You would think that public disengagement from democracy would be alarming to any politician or political party, but at least some political parties seem to want Canadians to opt out. Why? Because, perverse as it may seem in a democracy, it can bring the offending party an advantage. If a large segment of the population fails to vote, and many people in this segment support that party's opponents, it is to that party's advantage for them not to vote. Recent attempts by U.S. Republican Parties to restrict voter registration are a case in point.

And the longer I am involved in the political process, the more I believe the Conservative Party under Stephen Harper has been using similar tactics to deliberately reduce voter turnout.

Is this really what we as Canadians want for ourselves?

Whether by Machiavellian design or from voter cynicism, in the last federal election just slightly more than 60 per cent of those citizens entitled to vote actually did so. Voter turnout in our municipal elections is much worse—often as low as 20 per cent. Provincial election campaigns routinely have low voter turn-out. Alberta has the worst levels of participation, which reached its nadir in 2008, when only 41 per cent of those qualified to vote did so. In 2012 voter participation in Alberta increased in response to the tight race between Alison Redford's Progressive Conservatives and the upstart Wild-rose Party. Even then, the voter turnout was only 57 per cent.

But whatever we feel about politicians, we need good government. We need economic policies and goals that recognize the value and values of all Canadians. We need strong institutions that protect and preserve, not only our rights and privileges, but also, importantly, the patrimony of our lands and waters and the integrity of our environment. We need to both prepare and preserve for the future. We need to maximize the creative talents and potential of our youth and to encourage the natural abilities and inventiveness of Canadians through education and investment in their endeavours. We need to respect and protect the life work of our elders.

The Constitution does not mention the prime minister as part of government. It makes no reference to a PMO, the prime minister's office. The original BNA Act was premised on "peace, order and good government."

As humorist Arthur Black observes, "Two out of three ain't bad."[8]

We have something of a chicken and egg problem. We are experiencing a serious, pervasive assault on democracy, but only democracy can save us. Our ability to save ourselves is weakening—just when we need it most. The enormity of the climate crisis requires effective institutions and a robust response. Only in a democracy can the climate crisis be confronted effectively, while addressing social inequality. A fascist regime could act to reduce greenhouse gases, but I wouldn't want to be living in that society.

It is not too late to rescue democracy from politics. The way we talk about democracy conflates the idea of politics with democracy. But they are not the same thing. Politics and democracy are, while related, very different. Partisan politics, operating at the level of blood sport, is the sworn enemy of democracy, even as it parades in democracy's clothing. True, the word "politics" comes from the Greek word *polis*, meaning a city-state. From the early Athenian philosophers—Socrates, Plato, and Aristotle—came the first concepts of democracy.

For an Athenian, there was no way to separate democracy and the polis. As Alan Ryan observes in his brilliant and sweeping review of political thought, *On Politics*, an ancient Greek might not recognize the United States as a democracy—an observation that I am sure he would apply to Canada as well. According to Ryan:

> No Athenian believed that a Greek could be uninterested in politics. At the very least, self-defense demanded that a man keep a close eye on the holders of power; they understood what Trotsky observed twenty-five hundred years later. "You say you are not interested in politics; but politics is interested in you." The uninterest in politics and the ignorance about both politicians and political institutions displayed by British or American "citizens" of the present day would have been incomprehensible.[9]

Democracy has been contaminated by an unprecedented degree of partisanship. Media pundits and some politicians refer to politics as a "blood sport." It is treated like a game. But it is the lifeblood of democracy. And without a healthy, functioning democracy, how can we fix any of the other problems that affect our children's future?

The choices we make about economic models and goals are not value-neutral. They shape and drive cultural assumptions and society itself. To reinvigorate democracy, we need to encourage the kind of prosperity that rewards small and medium-sized businesses and innovators. We need to encourage a resilient, diverse, and robust economy with multitudes of players most likely to nurture a strong middle class. And a strong middle class is the *sine qua non* of a healthy democracy.

It stands to reason that if a petro-state linked to a petro-dollar reduces the manifestations of a healthy democracy, an economy organized around maximizing jobs, reducing the gap between the wealthiest and the poorest, and supporting a wide array of

171

burgeoning enterprises committed to research, development, and innovation, would have the opposite effect.

Where do we go from here? And if I can convince you to roll up your sleeves to help rescue democracy from politics, where would we start?

One problem I have seen clearly since I became an MP is that there is almost no institutional memory. New MPs assume the dim and oppressive atmosphere of modern-day Ottawa is normal. NDP and Liberal MPs don't seem to know any more than do Conservative MPs that it is quite wrong and a violation of our principles of parliamentary democracy to allow the PMO (or their leader's offices) to run everything. MPs assume their role is to do whatever their leader orders them to do and hope their constituents forgive them. No one seems to have read the Constitution and noted that the Prime Minister's Office and political parties are nowhere mentioned.

I worry that the next prime minister, regardless of political stripe, will happily maintain the oppressively tight reins of power once they hold them. The same unhealthy concentration of power is occurring in provincial governments. The power, once amassed, is not rebalanced toward democracy after the political banner has changed. In Nova Scotia, it was Progressive Conservative premier Rodney MacDonald who decreed that all deputy ministers should cease reporting through their ministers, bypass normal parliamentary practice, and report directly to the premier. This arrangement was maintained by incoming New Democratic premier Darrell Dexter, and the same is increasingly true in provincial capitals across Canada.

We are also sliding backwards in grounding our public policy choices in solid evidence.

172 To fix the sorry state of our parliamentary system, we need to focus attention on the unhealthy degree of power concentrated in the PMO, which is a relatively new invention. Until former prime minister Trudeau decided to have a larger staff to help coordinate

activities between and among cabinet members, the PMO was just a few secretaries and file clerks. It has grown to monstrous proportions, while remaining completely unaccountable. As a parliamentarian, I have been unable to get an exact count of how many people work there or what they earn. The PMO budget in 2011 topped $10 million, and all those funds are spent solely to promote the Conservative Party and enhance its chances of re-election.

We need to reduce the PMO budget and demand more transparency around its activities. In 2012, I proposed a 50 per cent cut in the PMO budget, but that's only a good start.

The PMO spin doctors should not be empowered to harass civil servants. Before Stephen Harper's time as prime minister, there was a fairly impervious wall between the civil service (the non-partisan bureaucracy) and the partisan elected ministers and their partisan staffs. If ministerial staffers wanted information from the department, they had to go through the deputy minister. If the prime minister wanted information, he or she had to go through the top boss of the civil service, the Clerk of the Privy Council. When Alex Himelfarb was Clerk of the Privy Council (essentially deputy minister to the Prime Minister's Office), he referred to the critical division between the PMO and the Privy Council Office (PCO) as a "Chinese firewall." Messages could pass between PMO and PCO, but the PCO could never be used as a tool of the political arm (the PMO).

It is a tricky relationship. Obviously, civil servants must take instructions and implement policy under different political masters. So when a civil service is under Progressive Conservative instructions from Brian Mulroney (or more accurately, Kim Campbell) one day, and then under Liberal Jean Chrétien the next, the civil service must pull together suitable advice and act according to instructions from the political masters.

What is not acceptable is for the PCO to "cook the books" to help buttress a political argument. The PCO has to stick to the

173

facts, not invent them for the government in power. Which is exactly what I think is now happening.

The firewall between the PMO and the PCO is down.

Public policy making is now only a shadow of good government. The outward appearance of a functional cabinet government supported by a non-partisan civil service is being maintained, but the reality is that nothing is normal. It reminds me of the scariest movie I ever saw: *Invasion of the Body Snatchers*, starring Donald Sutherland, in which pod people from outer space captured and genetically replicated humans. Friends looked the same but had become alien beings. Ottawa is experiencing a metaphorical alien invasion. Environment Canada may look like Environment Canada, but it's not. It's a pod department.

When I read reports prepared by Environment Canada claiming things that simply are not true (such as the statement in 2012 that we were "halfway" to our Copenhagen climate targets) in a report with numbers that prove the opposite, I smell political interference. Or when I read the Transport Canada report that was spun in the media to say the department had ruled supertankers carrying bitumen mixed with diluents could safely navigate the BC coastline, only to find that the report made no study of the specific hazards of the region, I smell political interference. And when Kevin Page, the first Parliamentary Budget Officer (PBO), could not get information about departmental spending from deputy ministers, the level of political interference reeks to high heaven. Even more shocking is that when the PBO went to the Federal Court of Canada and the court ruled that the PBO had a right to that information, the deputy ministers, no doubt under PMO orders, refused to release it. Despite the court ruling, at this writing, the deputies continue to refuse to hand over basic fiscal information to the office with the mandate to review the impacts of budgets.

Demonizing anyone in the civil service who stood for evidence-based decision making has also become routine, whether it be

174

Kevin Page, Parliamentary Budget Officer (reviled as incompetent), or Richard Colvin, the diplomat subpoenaed to testify about the torture of Afghan civilians (smeared as a Taliban stooge). Linda Keen was fired as head of the Canadian Nuclear Safety Commission for insisting the Chalk River reactor live up to its permit requirements. Munir Sheikh resigned on principle when his boss, Cabinet Minister Tony Clement, falsely claimed that his deputy minister and head statistician for Canada had never warned him that eliminating the long-form census would undermine the integrity of Statistics Canada data. Chief Electoral Officer Marc Mayrand was derided as though he were partisan, out to get the Conservative Party. Officers of the Crown and civil servants are increasingly muzzled and fearful.

Even more shocking was the criticism of the chief justice of the Supreme Court of Canada, with both the prime minister and minister of justice suggesting she had conducted herself inappropriately when no such thing was true.

The health of Canadian democracy continues to decline. As the Bruce Cockburn song has it, "The trouble with normal is it always gets worse."

PMO staff should not be allowed to bother individual civil servants, to tell them what to say or not to answer media inquiries. PMO staff should also not be allowed to bully members of parliament. Neither should MPs in opposition parties be dictated to by their leaders' offices. Members of parliament should be allowed—in fact, they should be encouraged—to represent their constituents. The Constitution of Canada says that MPs represent their constituencies. Working for political parties is never mentioned, because, of course, political parties are not mentioned in the Constitution at all.

I am often asked what has shocked me the most since I became a member of parliament. The biggest shock to me is that MPs do not read the legislation we are debating. Maybe some of them read some of it, but I am quite sure I am the only MP who

175

reads all of it. In spring 2012, during the horrific passage of the omnibus budget bill C-38 without a single change, most cabinet ministers who spoke to the bill had not read it. The people who wrote their speeches could not have read it. That is how Ministers Kent and Oliver, as well as parliamentary secretaries, were able to keep referring to things in the bill that were not there. When I would go to any of the ministers privately to ask them to show me where the steps they claimed were in the bill could be found, they would at first attempt a bluff. "Well, Elizabeth, it's a very big bill." And then I would say, "I know. I have read it. But I cannot find any reference to [fill in the blank—improved tanker safety, pipeline inspections...]." I would watch their faces fall, and then they would recover with a game "It must be something coming in subsequent regulations."

I decided to have some sport with this reality to make a point. I offered a prize to any MP who could complete a simple multiple-choice quiz on the bill—and the quiz would be "open book." The whole text would be available for reference. Not a single Conservative MP accepted the challenge. The only MP who did was Independent Bruce Hyer (Thunder Bay–Superior North), formerly an NDP MP. He passed with flying colours. (And he now sits as a Green MP.)

Since I was making an issue of the fact that no one seemed to have read the bill, during debate one backbench Conservative MP boasted that he had read the whole thing. But he blew his credibility when he added, "What can I say? I like numbers."

Because it was called the omnibus budget bill, he must have thought it was four hundred–plus pages of numbers. If he had even flipped through the pages, he would have seen nothing but text. The only numbers were the section and subsection headings.

I have come to understand why MPs, in all parties, don't read the bills. Why bother if you are going to be instructed how to vote and punished if you do not follow your instructions? I have always known there are things called "whipped votes." I even knew that, occasionally, past prime ministers would use a whip to force votes a certain way in parliamentary committees. What I had not understood until I was elected was that every vote is now a whipped vote.

The pages, those bright young university students in their black tailored parliamentary uniforms (a look made famous by Brigette DePape holding up her STOP HARPER sign), move quietly through the chamber while the bell sounds to signify a coming vote. For most votes, there are thirty minutes of bells. While the bells ring, the House is not in session. Most MPs are not in their seats, and the pages peer carefully at the names on the side of the desks to avoid error. It would be a large-scale error to hand the voting instructions for one party to MPs in another party. Every day on every vote, the instruction sheets from Conservative, NDP, Liberal, and Bloc Québécois whips are placed on the desks of their respective MPs.

One day, as a Liberal colleague was reviewing his instructions, he looked up at me and joked, "Gee, Elizabeth, how do you know how to vote?"

When you are instructed how to vote, what possible benefit could there be in reading the legislation and actually deciding for yourself? All it could do would be to make an MP who disagreed with the bill even unhappier and more disempowered. It was hard to be the only MP to vote against the continued aerial bombardment of Libya in June 2011. It would have been even harder to be one of the NDP peace activist MPs forced to vote with the Conservatives and bombing. A number came up to me afterwards with tears in their eyes to congratulate me on my vote. Conservative MPs also expressed their disgust when forced to vote that asbestos is safe. One said in a confessional whisper, "I am going to go home now and have a shower because I have never felt so dirty in all my life."

MPs in caucuses with strong party discipline—and that seems to be all the others—can be severely punished for voting in defiance of their instructions. Punishments in a caucus where its leader is also the prime minister are the harshest; the leader has access to more perks to withdraw. The most extreme measures open to a prime minister are illustrated in the case of Helena Guergis. Her expulsion from Cabinet and banishment from caucus to the hinterland as an Independent MP all started because of a relatively innocuous incident at the Charlottetown airport, when she was delayed at security in Charlottetown and asked to remove her boots. It was reported that she behaved in ways that are unacceptable for a cabinet minister, swearing and saying that she couldn't wait to get out of Charlottetown, which she described in unprintable fashion. It was her birthday and it was reported that, as she threw her boots in the bin for screening, she said, "Happy f—king birthday to me."

Charlottetown is a small-enough place that word of the incident spread quickly. People knew she was a cabinet minister, and her behaviour was over the top. I found out later that she had recently had a miscarriage, so I felt a great deal of sympathy for her. Having had a few myself, I know your emotions are raw and hormones at their craziest after the blow. Guergis had not thwarted the prime minister; she had just become embarrassing to him.

At first, Stephen Harper defended her. He should have explained to her that she had to leave Cabinet. For much less, a Progressive Conservative member of Mulroney's Cabinet had had to resign. Alan Redman had made a joke about guns in the airport security lineup. He admitted he had been a fool and apologized, losing his cabinet post in the process. But Stephen Harper would not admit there was any reason for her to step aside, and the story simply wouldn't go away. For one thing, it appeared that her husband, another former Conservative MP, Rahim Jaffer, had been using her office to promote his own business interests. And there were more allegations coming to light about him.

My own theory is that because Harper can never admit he made a mistake, he couldn't demand her resignation for a matter he had initially dismissed. And he had made it a point of pride not to allow his cabinet members to resign. As leader of the Opposition back in the day, he had crowed about forcing the resignation of a Liberal cabinet member over a minor matter. He knew the Opposition wanted to force ministers out to collect points against the boss. So when he finally decided Guergis was a liability, he not only fired her from his Cabinet but threw her out of the Conservative backbenches to boot. Harper accused her of doing something so inappropriate and potentially illegal that he was calling on the RCMP and the Ethics Commissioner to investigate.

The Ethics Commissioner found there was nothing to investigate. So did the RCMP. Her reputation in tatters at the hands of her former boss, Guergis went to court. The court ruled that it could not adjudicate her claims against Harper and the Conservative Party as his actions were covered by parliamentary privilege and the prime minister's use of prerogative power. It said it could not inject itself into the relationship between a prime minister and cabinet members.

When I was elected, Helena phoned to ask if I would consider hiring a young woman who had been on her staff. Given that her staff had had to cope with being ousted from a party structure and to figure out for themselves how to function in the House of Commons working for an Independent MP, Helena argued persuasively that her former staffer would be a real asset for me. I felt awful, because I had already hired my staff and we had such a tiny budget there was no way to even consider adding another staffer. But I offered a hopeful "I am sure with all the newly elected Conservative MPs, she won't have any trouble finding another job."

"No," said Helena sadly, "she's been told she is blacklisted because she worked for me."

That level of pettiness and vindictiveness made it clear. Punishment in this system is total and merciless.

What an object lesson in total punishment to other MPs and cabinet members. Nothing was even alleged against Helena Guergis remotely justifying the assault on her reputation.

How is it that leaders of parties can dictate to members of parliament how they should vote, what they should say, and when they should say nothing at all? The power to make effective threats and to enforce party discipline was due to a rather innocuous change in our Canada Elections Act. Or, at least it seemed innocuous at the time.

Before the late 1960s, the names of candidates appeared on the ballot without any mention of the party for which they stood. Elections Canada reviewed the growing size of ridings (now called electoral district associations) and the increasing likelihood that voters would not know the names of the people running for office. To aid in voter information, it was decided to put the name of the candidate's party on the ballot. That created another small problem: What if a candidate claimed to represent a party that, in fact, had no connection to the candidate? To avoid that hypothetical problem, the Canada Elections Act was changed to require the party leader's signature on every nomination form, specifically approving each of that party's candidates.

Without intending to do so, the changed elections law handed the leaders of political parties their first effective bludgeon to keep candidates, and MPs, in line. A leader can threaten to pull, or refuse to sign, the signed nomination papers from any candidate. We need to fix this. We need to ensure that a local riding association can select the candidate. The leader's signature should not be required. We need to liberate MPs to do the job described in the Constitution: represent their constituents.

The link between MPs and their constituents has been more politicized by Stephen Harper than by any other prime minister. Traditionally it was understood that when the government of Canada made an announcement anywhere in Canada, the MP for that community was automatically invited. Harper does the opposite. Opposition MPs not only are prevented from speaking at such events but are not made aware of the announcement at all. The dispensing of government funding is reserved for Conservative

MPS, as though the general revenues of the government of Canada are taken from the Conservative Party's bank account. In fact, one recent government press release announced that "Prime Minister Stephen Harper" was funding a local project.

A prime minister in Canada has more power than the president of the U.S. or the British prime minister. In the U.S., the president is restricted by a system of checks and balances created by revolutionaries deeply suspicious of abuse of power, and in the UK, the prime minister must deal with a purer system of Westminster parliamentary democracy than in Canada. In contrast, a Canadian prime minister can be a virtual dictator. We have morphed toward a presidential prime ministerial role, while leaders in all parties have amassed excessive power. The election of leaders by political party membership and rules that say only the members can remove a leader have given a Canadian prime minister more power than leaders in any other Commonwealth nation.

In the rest of the Commonwealth, those countries with Westminster parliamentary systems, a leader, including a prime minister, can be deposed by the sitting caucus of that party's MPS. That is how former prime minister Margaret Thatcher was removed and, more recently, how former prime minister Kevin Rudd of Australia was replaced by former prime minister Julia Gillard, who was then replaced when Rudd engineered another caucus revolt and a return to power.

Excessive power in the backrooms of political parties is a direct threat to a healthy democracy.

One of the things I love about the Green Party is that, despite Elections Canada rules empowering me to act in dictatorial fashion, the party's internal rules do not allow me to reject a candidate unilaterally. It is something of a Green Party tradition to resist hyper-partisanship. As German Green Party founder Petra Kelly once said, "We are the anti-party party." If I could get rid of political parties, I would. I think it would improve democracy.[10]

To encourage more Canadians to vote, we need to make the democratic process more engaging. We need to ensure that casting a vote is an empowering experience. The best way to do that is to get rid of first past the post.

The system by which Canadians elect their MPs was invented more than a thousand years ago. Of the modern democracies, only Canada, the U.S., and the UK still use first past the post (FPTP). All the others use some form of proportional representation. Elections Canada has done a lot of research, as have other democracies, on what increases voter turnout. It is something called the "efficacy" of your vote. If you are in a room of ten people voting on which one of the ten will get to chair a prestigious process, you are very likely to vote. Your vote will count.

The most disempowering aspect of FPTP is the feeling that your vote will not count. As soon as one candidate has more votes than any of the others, even when that "winning" number is far less than the majority of votes cast, all the votes for other candidates are discarded. Fair Vote Canada, an organization dedicated to changing our voting system, refers to all those votes cast for candidates who did not win as orphan votes. The essence of proportional representation is to ensure that every vote counts. No vote is thrown out. No orphan vote is left behind.

There are a number of ways to engineer a proportional representation system. There is mixed member proportional (MMP), which includes a representative for each local district, but also sets seats aside to ensure that Parliament as a whole reflects the actual percentage of votes cast for each party. This is the most common system, used in much of Europe and in New Zealand. Another type of system uses a single transferable vote (STV), in which a group of ridings are clustered together and voters are allowed to cast a number of ballots, ranked in preference. A voter only gets one vote (a single vote), but it is transferable insofar that as soon as your number one choice has secured a seat, your vote moves to the second choice and so on through a cluster of ridings in one area. Lastly, there is pure proportional representation, where your vote is not attached to any local representation. This is a very rare and in my view undesirable system. Only Italy and Israel use this system.

Making sure every vote counts is a fundamental part of a healthy democracy, and either MMP or STV would be an enormous improvement on FPTP.

There is a pretty reliable prescription to fix what ails our sick system. It starts with a good old-fashioned dose of public engagement. As Tom Robbins wrote in *Still Life with Woodpecker:* "Life is like a stew, you have to stir it frequently, or all the scum rises to the top."[11]

A Holiday from the Facts

A happy, hardworking, goods-consuming citizen [is] perfect... Otherwise the wheels stop turning... You're so conditioned that you can't help doing what you ought to do. And what you ought to do is on the whole so pleasant... that there really aren't any temptations to resist. And if ever, by some unlucky chance, anything unpleasant should somehow happen, why, there's always [the drug] soma... to make you patient and long-suffering, to give you a holiday from the facts.

ALDOUS HUXLEY, *Brave New World*[12]

Chapter Ten

MOVING FROM OBSERVER TO PARTICIPANT

Y OU MAY REMEMBER the book about the man who laughed himself well. If you are old enough and have a very good memory, you may remember Ed Asner playing the famous editor of the *Saturday Review of Literature* in a 1984 TV movie. Norman Cousins, whose 1979 book *Anatomy of an Illness: As Perceived by the Patient* inspired the film, was my adopted uncle. He met my mom when she had the chutzpah to arrange a meeting with the icon of literature and of the peace movement to ask whether he agreed with her that nuclear weapons testing should be illegal. They became friends, and through that friendship, Norman's sister Jeannie married my mom's big brother, Tom Middleton.

It was an early and traumatic event in my childhood when Norman nearly died in 1964. He had been in Moscow for meetings, ingesting a great deal of pollution, as diesel trucks spewed toxic air through his open hotel window in a very hot city. A combination of factors, other infections and stress, contributed to a devastating illness. By the time he was back in New York, his connective tissue was mysteriously swelling. The diagnosis was ankylosing spondylitis, an inflammatory disease of the spine. He blew up like a balloon. Thinking Norman was asleep, the attending physician, who was one of his best friends, said softly to another friend, "I think we are going to lose Norman."

"It was at that point," Norman wrote, "that I decided to take an interest in the case."

Using the resources of his research staff, he discovered a depressed immune system was a factor in his illness. When he learned that stress depressed the immune system, he reasoned that laughter and joy must be good for it. He also reasoned that a hospital was no place for a sick person and he moved into a nearby hotel. Given the U.S. medical system in 1964, a room at the Mayflower Hotel and a round-the-clock nurse were less expensive than the hospital. Then he rented a movie projector and his nurse's main job became running Marx Brothers movies and episodes of *Candid Camera*. When he ran out of funny movies, he had her run them backwards. My mom's visit to his hotel room may also have contributed to his recovery.

She had driven herself to Manhattan from Hartford with an assortment of fears. She was nervous about visiting a man in a hotel room—even a very sick man. She was afraid of walking in and out of a parking garage in New York City. And she was afraid of allowing a very political letter to fall into the wrong hands.

The world's leading intellectuals, in an effort organized by Lord Bertrand Russell, had decided to send an open letter urging Americans to defeat Barry Goldwater. Once before, Lord Russell had given my mother an unpublished manuscript. For completely different reasons, she had also given it to Norman.

She received the first Bertrand Russell manuscript when she visited him at his home in Wales. Well into his eighties, he had bounded up the stairs two at a time as she followed him to his study. "Here is my *History of the World for Martian Infant Schools*," he had said as he gave her his manuscript.

It was a single sheet of paper upon which he had written "Ever since Adam ate the apple, man has refrained from no folly of which he was capable. The End."

Norman had loved the quote and titled a book he had just completed on the threat of nuclear war *In Place of Folly*.

Now she had a sheet of paper of a different kind. Bertrand Russell had thought it a good idea to warn the American public of the threat posed by Barry Goldwater to world peace. His manifesto in favour of Lyndon Johnson had been signed by the most brilliant and celebrated of Europe's brainiest brains. When my mother saw the letter, she was horrified that many of the signatories were Communists. She was sure that if the letter were ever made public, Barry Goldwater would win the election.

She didn't want it to fall into the wrong hands. And the only way she could see to persuade Lord Russell to abandon his plan was to have Hubert Humphrey, LBJ's running mate, phone him directly to explain tactfully that, as well intentioned as was the effort, it would be best incinerated. And the only way she knew to get Humphrey to make such a call was to have Norman phone Humphrey.

My mother struggled with what else to take Norman besides a deeply dangerous manifesto. Chocolates were out—too unhealthy. Flowers for his room were also a bad idea—Norman had allergies and was prone to hay fever. She ended up buying a very realistic and expensive vase of fake roses, which were awkward and had to be held at arm's length.

To combat potential rapists and muggers in the parking garage, she bought a super-loud alarm, set off by pulling a string, which yanked a pin out of a small device.

As she walked into the hotel lobby, holding the vase of fake flowers out in front of her, manuscript tucked under one arm, she noticed her purse wasn't closed. She snapped it shut with her elbow, and in doing so accidentally pulled the string that released the pin and set off the alarm. The device was very effective and very alarming. An ear-piercing automated shriek rang out and the hotel lobby erupted into panic. People ran in circles or raced to exits while staff tried to verify if there was a fire.

187

My mom couldn't reach the purse or the pin until she had walked through the lobby with as much calm and lady-like grace as she could muster, struggling to maintain some dignity. When she reached the reception desk, she set down the plastic floral display and, with trembling hands, replaced the pin in the anti-rape device. Then very calmly, she said, "Mr. Cousins's room, please."

When she told Norman the story, he laughed so hard that I'm sure it helped speed his recovery. As he wrote later, a solid belly laugh was worth several hours of uninterrupted drug-free sleep. And he made her leave the anti-rape noisemaker with him so he could tell the story to other visitors and pull the pin out for full effect, leaving her to face her fears of lurking muggers in the parking garage unalarmed. Norman phoned Hubert Humphrey and the European communist campaign for LBJ was aborted.

And Norman lived on, writing *Anatomy of an Illness* fifteen years later.

I keep thinking of that understated line from Norman when he heard his doctor say, "I think we are going to lose Norman": "It was at that point that I decided to take an interest in the case."

In speaking about the threats to our democracy and the related threats to our survival because of the climate crisis, I often use the analogy of a medical diagnosis. What are the vital signs for our democracy? Could our democracy pass a stress test? Are we as a society in robust health? We have a serious addiction problem. We are addicted to fossil fuels and despite warnings that we must adopt healthier choices, we persist in a dangerous addiction.

We are collectively in a desperate state of ill health, in terms of our societal health, our democracy, and the clear diagnosis that our future (and, increasingly, our present) is being imperilled by the climate crisis.

And yet we lie there. When will we take an interest in the case? When will we move from observer to our own worrying diagnosis and become active participants? When will we start the process of saving our own lives?

The situation may seem hopeless, but it is not. We will change things if we believe we can. Strong, positive, and committed people are needed. Cynicism and despair are our enemies.

We do not lack data, science, or technology. We do not lack economic solutions that will improve our overall prosperity. We do not lack policies. We lack the will to make it happen. We lack political will, from our leaders and from ourselves.

Politicians bear the brunt of the responsibility for our political disengagement. Our political culture is a toxic swamp, turning citizens off politics. But there are other factors. Part of the reason for our disengagement lies in our extremely comfortable lifestyle. We are privileged. We are also inundated with consumerism. That 1955 marketing journal has proved prophetic. We are distracted by shopping as our core ritualistic activity. We have allowed ourselves to be described as consumers, and only rarely as citizens.

We are bombarded with advertising from dawn to dusk to tell us which beer or bottled water to drink, what new gadget to buy. We are swept up in a maelstrom of consumer enticements. And to some extent, we are addicted to them. The addictions (our coffee, our alcohol, our prescription drugs, our illegal drugs, our shopping habit) serve to anaesthetize us to the bigger questions: Why are we here? What is the meaning of life? What is the meaning of my life in particular? Will I make a difference?

Where will we find that energy for change? How do we overcome the cognitive dissonance between our knowledge that Canada is in trouble and our failure to accept personal responsibility and do anything about it?

Perhaps we need to address this as a moral and spiritual crisis. To paraphrase Einstein, it won't be enough to use the tools that created the problem to get out of it. We need a broader, deeper, more empowering analysis.

189

I found great inspiration in working on the Earth Charter in 1997. Through some fluke I was selected to work in a group of about two dozen extraordinary world citizens—the late Mercedes

Sosa, the brilliant Argentinian singer; Leonardo Boff, Brazilian theologian; Princess Basma of Jordan, sister of the late King Hussein; former presidents and prime ministers from Mali and the Netherlands; and other activists, including Kenyan environmentalist and winner of the Nobel Peace Prize the late Wangari Maathai, and youth activist Severn Cullis-Suzuki, David and Tara's daughter, whom I had known since she was five.

We all gathered in a hotel room in Rio de Janeiro five years after the Earth Summit. It was the Rio Plus 5 Conference, and we had come to finalize a text for the Earth Charter. Our small group was chaired by Mikhail Gorbachev. He regaled us with stories of how he picked up the phone, over the objections of his officials, and personally put it to Ronald Reagan, "Do you want to eliminate all nuclear weapons? Because I do." And Reagan agreed.

It was a revelation to have the former leader of what I had been brought up to believe was a godless Communist country urge us to find the words to help the Earth Charter be as inspiring as the Sermon on the Mount. One of the greatest insights came from the representative from India, the late Kamla Chowdhry, who had worked with Gandhi. She urged us to make the point that "*having more can never replace being more.*"

This isn't just about voting or changing the kind of light bulbs we use. It is about a change at the level of our hearts and our faith. We cannot inspire change by talking about a carbon tax, even though that is what we need. We cannot empower a political renaissance merely by pointing out that the current ruling party is dominated by an ideology that rejects science or evidence.

You cannot move people to change simply by railing against what's wrong. We need to move people to change by describing how much better it could be. The potential for a healthier economy, the reduced gap between the wealthiest and the poorest, a strong middle class—all of this is possible.

The benefits to society as a whole of ensuring that persistent poverty is eradicated are well documented. One of the best

190

studies of how an egalitarian, equitable society provides a higher quality of life for all is Kate Pickett and Richard Wilkinson's *The Spirit Level—Why Greater Equality Makes Societies Stronger.* Just as Canadian visionary Jane Jacobs had often described, a society where people are willing to reach out and help each other and to recognize a neighbour on the street, even if it is a nodding acquaintance, makes for a stronger, more resilient society. The evidence of deaths in heat waves confirms that the greater the fear and isolation, the higher the casualties. Resilient communities start with social networks.

It was an unsung advantage of my old neighbourhood in Ottawa. I knew my neighbours. That knowing my neighbours was unusual elsewhere was brought home to me when a wonderful young lawyer from the Washington office of the Natural Resources Defense Council visited me in 2001.

We were working to stop a Canadian company from building a dam in Belize, a dam that would threaten a rich and diverse ecosystem, habitat to many endangered species. We had eaten dinner, and my daughter thought cookies would be a good idea. Ari and I continued talking and considering strategy while I grabbed ingredients off the shelf and started mixing. I was well into the process when I reached into the fridge for eggs and discovered that we didn't have any. "Back in a sec," I said over my shoulder as I dashed out the back door, crossed the street, and knocked on Barb's door to ask for two eggs. I breezed back into the kitchen, having barely missed a minute's conversation, continuing mid-sentence. But the look on Ari's face stopped me. "Did you just go across the street and get eggs from a neighbour?" he asked. "You know your neighbours?" I nodded and he continued, "I've seen that sort of thing on TV, but I didn't think it happened in real life."

As we talked about this, I found that not only did he not know a single neighbour where he lived in Washington, he had not known any of the neighbours in the suburban community outside

San Diego where he grew up either. I had been taking for granted a significant amount of my quality of life.

We need to advocate for resilient communities. A healthy community is not necessarily a wealthy neighbourhood, though it could be. It would likely have greater density and diversity as well as varying incomes, most hovering somewhere around the middle class mark.

We can work to solve two societal problems at once. A carbon charge structured as a carbon fee and dividend will reduce pollution while at the same time distributing funds to every citizen. This will disproportionately benefit the poorest. It is possible to eliminate poverty, and a carbon fee and dividend ensures the return of funds collected from polluters to each and every Canadian.

Another thing that we can work toward in a better future will be a more sensible pace of life. We need to address economic poverty, but we also need to address poverty of time.

Statistics Canada keeps track (or used to before Harper killed the long-form census) of Canadians' sense of whether we have enough time to do all the tasks we are pressed to complete. You will not be surprised to learn that most Canadians—but particularly working mothers, and even more so working single mothers—never feel they have enough time to complete essential tasks. Dr. Ron Coleman of GPI Atlantic, based in Halifax, has a term for this condition. He calls it "time poverty."

We have too much stuff in our lives, but the economy demands that we keep buying, wasting, chewing it up, and spitting it out. We need two incomes to keep our heads above water. Our homes are larger, but fewer of us are able to afford one. We are on an economic treadmill. And we sorely lack time.

192 Studies have shown that longer commuting times are directly linked to a decline in volunteer activity. Commuting time has increased across Canada. For frustrating gridlock, Toronto scores the highest. Statistics Canada reports that in 1992 Canadians

commuted an average of fifty-four minutes daily and that in 2011, we were up to an average of sixty-two minutes a day. The Federation of Canadian Municipalities points out that all those minutes spent getting from home to work and back add up to an average of thirty-two days a year per employee. That's thirty-two days of lost productivity per person at a cost of $10 billion a year.

One of my best friends from my Cape Breton days has resettled in White Rock, BC, where she runs a licensed day care centre out of her home. Many people who work in Vancouver end up living in White Rock because of its lower housing costs and higher quality of life. But their commute is brutal. I have stayed at Liz's place when children, still half-asleep, are dropped off before 7 AM to have breakfast with Liz and then go off to school and then at the end of the day come back to her house for after-school activities until their stressed-out parents, who have been calling from their car to say the traffic is really bad, make it back to her house to collect the kids around dinnertime. Those kids clock a long day— sometimes over twelve hours without seeing their parents. The whole family is stressed out throughout the work week.

And then on weekends, we don't give ourselves a break. My own stepkids are hockey parents, and getting ice time at the rink is a priority. So there's no such thing as sleeping late on a Saturday. Mass transit doesn't work well when you have to muscle a hockey bag onto the subway, so they drive in Toronto morning traffic. Watching them on weekends makes me even happier that, when my daughter was growing up, I didn't own a car.

My car, which I sold in 1980 to pay my phone bill, was the last one I owned until 2007, when being leader of the Green Party (ironically) meant I had to have a car to get around and campaign. For all of my daughter's formative years, we walked or took the bus. I remember when one of her elementary school friends was coming home with us for a sleepover. As we walked out of the school, Victoria Cate's friend asked, "Where did you park the car?" Victoria Cate said, "We don't have a car." Undaunted, her friend asked,

"Where is your van?" "We don't have a van," said Victoria Cate. Her friend was starting to sound panicked as we kept on walking. "What do you have?" Victoria Cate said, "We have our feet."

Not owning a car was, by my lights, a huge blessing. I saved a large amount of money by not owning a car—money I felt justified in spending on an annual holiday. And walking with my daughter, hand in hand, to and from school, was the best time of any day. Uninterrupted by phone calls or emails, we could walk silently or talk about whatever crossed our minds. As we walked, I would tell her what plant species we were passing. We would talk about the animals we saw. Anything at all, at the lovely pace of a stroll, could be the topic of conversation. Any time she came to me with a suggested activity—usually a dance or art class—I would figure out how we could manage the travel. If it was an activity that required a car, she understood that it just wouldn't work. I spared myself a lot of stress from driving in traffic by simply not having the option.

Fortunately, the enriching extracurricular activities of her childhood were found within walking distance. Some of them were right in our own kitchen. I cooked every meal from scratch. It saved money and gave me confidence in what she was eating. Our meals were organic, locally sourced as much as possible, and vegetarian. Every Sunday afternoon, I made bread for the week with organic whole wheat flour. In addition to shaving pennies off the food budget, making my own bread gave me some quiet time for writing, between the brief bursts of activity to punch down and knead the loaves. I had my laptop at one end of the kitchen table while bread rose at the other end.

I never enrolled my daughter in cooking classes, but she can look up a recipe on the internet and whip up a soufflé or whatever comes to mind. For Christmas holidays recently, I made my favourite Italian desert, zabaglione, using a large number of egg yolks. To avoid waste, Victoria Cate made meringues with the whites. When she was in grade school and I was a single mother running a national environmental organization and working long days and usually on weekends, I had ample excuses to say I didn't have time to cook. But cooking enhances my sense of well-being. I love being around good food and love serving a home-cooked meal. Cooking every meal created less stress than sticking pizza pops in a microwave. And, anyway, I didn't own a microwave.

Not everyone enjoys cooking, but my hunch is that if more people knew how to cook, they would enjoy it. As we become increasingly deficient in basic life skills, we are becoming more and more dependent on the processed food industry and its "convenience" products—overpackaged, additive- and chemical-laden, nutritionally eroded garbage masquerading as food. Meanwhile, farmers cannot make a living growing our food, and the infrastructure of local agriculture is being dismantled all around us. We have lost our local canneries, our slaughterhouses, our dairies. The globally competitive agri-business model prefers mega-hog barns, massive slaughterhouses, and a growth trajectory premised on exports. The fact that Canadian farmers cannot earn a living and have to take off-farm work to make ends meet is of no concern. The carbon miles attached to imported garlic from China are also irrelevant. Garlic grows well everywhere in southern Canada, but most of the major grocery chains still import it. The model is flawed and our access to healthy, local foods is compromised.

No matter what a politician tells you, the goal of Canadian regulators is not safe food for Canadians. The goal is expanded export and market share for ersatz food-stuff. Canadian governments, federally and provincially, focus on corporate profits, not seeking food security or well-being and good health through food.

Just as convenience foods have eroded the art of cooking, so have they enabled everyone to eat at different times. Eating meals together as a family is practically a thing of the past. We think we are saving time this way, though we are depriving ourselves of family time.

And where does that "saved" time go? Nowhere anyone can find it. Families keep losing out on time together. Church groups lament that youth sports started having early Sunday morning practices. A few decades ago, Sunday mornings were off limits, and even families not attending church could spend Sunday mornings together. No longer.

How much time we have for family meals, spending time together, putting our feet up at the end of the day—all ignored by the Gross Domestic Product (GDP). So we run ourselves ragged to keep the economy going, even as we sense that this isn't the life we had in mind.

Ron Coleman has done a lot of work in the Kingdom of Bhutan, which has a measure called Gross Domestic Happiness. We had a wonderful conference in Antigonish, Nova Scotia, a few years back, organized by Ron and his wife, Gwen, on the concept of Gross Domestic Happiness. Amazing speakers like Ray Anderson from Interface and representatives from Bhutan shared their experiences. It was an eye-opening exploration of how we might go about measuring things that matter. And one of those things is the sense of personal empowerment that comes from knowing you make a difference in your society.

Personal political engagement is a source of improved morale, stronger self-worth, and even happiness. But we are running so hard that many of us think being involved in the community is just one thing too many.

So, at least one of the factors in our disengagement with politics is our culture and lifestyle.

We need to push for the four-day work week, creating more jobs—part-time, flex-time, home telecommuting—to make our lives richer and more enjoyable. We need to keep remembering that having more can never replace being more.

So how do we then become more politically engaged?

We need an informed and active citizenry.

Unfortunately, it is difficult to become informed in the face of our weak, resource-deprived media. Nearly all Canada's newspapers, radio stations, and television networks are owned by a handful of corporate players. The national public broadcasters, the CBC and Radio-Canada, are exceptions, but they are afraid of losing funding and so are also increasingly timid. The forty-two daily newspapers in Canada owned by Postmedia carry syndicated news and columns. We had a golden opportunity when the Canwest empire melted down and the forty-two newspapers in its chain were up for sale. Tragically, the trustee in bankruptcy insisted all forty-two be sold as a block. It was the perfect time to give some entrepreneur who loves journalism a chance to bring the *Kingston Whig-Standard* and the *London Free Press* back to their glory days. I was the only political leader to call for the government to dismantle the corporate control of all forty-two major dailies, and, in the end, Postmedia picked them up. This is not to say that there is never a great article or serious reporting in Postmedia papers. They often contain impressive pieces of work, such as the exposés on the election fraud by robo-calls and paid live calls on 2011 election day to defraud the voter, written by Glenn McGregor and Stephen Maher. Margaret Munro and Mike De Souza of Postmedia have also provided excellent coverage of the environment, but Postmedia has laid off most of its Parliament Hill team, including Mike De Souza.

The result is an inadequate level of coverage and analysis. Generally speaking, most local coverage deals with sports and not the local city council debates. National coverage is composed of cookie cutter articles from the national service.

New research shows that, when a local newspaper lays off its Ottawa reporter, voter turnout in federal elections declines in that community.[1]

Concentration of ownership is staggering. The *Globe and Mail* and CTV *National News* are both owned by Bell, with vertically integrated media, telecommunications, and related enterprises. Shaw owns Global TV, and Sun Media, a subsidiary of Quebecor, owns the Sun chain, much of the Quebec daily press, and the Sun television network.

Back in the 1960s, the late Tom Kent headed a royal commission studying the concentration of ownership in Canadian media. He reported that the degree of monopoly ownership was "monstrous" and that it was a threat to democracy. Fifty years later it is markedly worse, and we no longer even talk about it.

So what do we do? Between elections, we can at least take the time to share concerns with other Canadians through letters to the editor. The letters page is the most read section of any newspaper. Becoming informed as active citizens by reading widely, we can share that knowledge within our communities through letters to the editor. We can increase awareness of the threats the media is no longer covering.

A letter to the editor accomplishes multiple goals. It increases public awareness of an issue and informs the newspaper of local interest for that issue. And every letter is clipped by the service to let every minister in every portfolio read about public concerns. A published letter to the editor is a very effective tool.

It is also useful to spend time in the comment sections of online media sites. It is like weeding a garden; the trolls will take over if you are not attending to the conversation, supporting those comments that are accurate about climate science and calling out as nonsense those that promote a fossil fuel future. The *Guardian*'s George Monbiot discovered that fossil fuel lobbyists in the UK were using such comment sites to promote their agenda. Comments are anonymous and unverified, so a single industry lobbyist with multiple IP addresses can create the false sense that there is public sympathy for a particular agenda. One of their tactics is to be personally abusive. The ad hominem abuse is designed to drive away the average concerned citizen. Being subjected to public ridicule is hard for nice people, so the industry flacks can disproportionately dominate such sites. Balancing such propaganda with the views of real (and respectful) citizen comment is a huge public service. We need active citizens to take on this task.

We need to advocate for a healthy news media with a range of voices. We must support the local media. In every community across Canada, there is a small local newspaper. Usually, they are weeklies or even biweeklies. In an age of the corporate control of the mainstream press and the craven cowardice of our national public broadcaster, often it is a small local paper, clinging to its economic viability by a thread, that informs and inspires. We need to read and buy our little local newspapers. Often they are the only place left where the free flow of ideas can take place in the non-virtual public square.

Over the years, the small papers I have read and to which I have occasionally contributed articles have really helped increase local awareness of burning issues. And the contributors and editors are often committed to a high standard of journalism.

In my riding, there is a great little magazine, called *Focus*, that often covers issues other larger publications miss. And there is an extraordinary independent local paper, *Island Tides*, which mixes local, regional, national, and international news. *Island Tides'* strength is that it is a regional newspaper and circulates on all the islands in the Strait of Georgia and parts of Vancouver Island, over a 120-mile strip. Through publishing ideas and actions and giving the west coast of Vancouver Island a progressive voice over the last quarter-century, it has aided in the development of an exceptionally informed electorate, willing to take action. Other communities across Canada boast of similar local newspapers.

There are also many superb online newspapers. Here in British Columbia, the *Tyee* is excellent. Nationally we have *iPolitics* and *Rabble.ca*. The *Huffington Post* is often helpful in raising awareness of issues, but, unfortunately, it does not pay its contributors. For freelance writers, life is hard enough without a newspaper that offers bloggers a byline but no payment.

Never forget that for the major media outlets, you can make a difference if you complain. My brother has proved this to me over and over again. Even though he is isolated in a tiny community on Cape Breton Island, he is a media hound and watchdog. And he does not let our beloved CBC off the hook. Once he heard a 6 AM CBC national news radio broadcast that contained a whopping error about climate change. (The newscast had mentioned the East Anglia hacked emails—referring to them as "leaks"—as proof that there was fraud in climate science.) Since he knew that this newscast was being heard at 5 AM in Ontario, he reasoned that there was time to fix the error before the story was aired again. He phoned CBC Toronto and left a message on the listener feedback line that the story needed to be corrected. For good measure, he left a similar message on the newsroom voicemail. And then he waited. The story remained unchanged at 7 AM, and so he phoned again.

At 8 AM the story was still unchanged, but when he phoned the newsroom, he got a real live person. Maybe it was his intensity and the fact that he had phoned several times. The voice on the other end of the phone asked if he wanted to speak to the CBC reporter who had filed the story. "But isn't she in London?" Geoff asked. "Yes, but we'll patch you through." The next thing he knew he was speaking to the reporter in the UK. She was actually grateful to know she had made a mistake and she promised to correct it. She had not had time to find out the details about the hacked emails. She wasn't sure about the leaking versus hacking part of the story, and she didn't know there was no evidence the scientists had been fudging data. Finally, she asked about my brother's background. University professor? "No," he said. "I'm *nobody*, but I pay attention and I worry when the national news is spouting stuff that I know isn't true." So should we all.

We need to revive a healthy news media to ensure a functioning democracy. We need to ensure enhanced, stable funding for our national public broadcaster.

We must ensure that in election campaigns all party leaders are pressed to respond to concerns about the democratic deficit. We need to encourage all the parties to commit to reforms, particularly the easy ones. While reforming the Senate gets most of the attention, tackling any meaningful change in that body requires opening up the Constitution. But, without opening the Constitution, we can eliminate the first past the post voting system and bring in proportional representation. It will take only a vote in the House and the Senate.

We can slash the budget of the PMO. Cutting it in half would be a good start. We can amend the Elections Act to remove the requirement for the leader's signature on nomination forms, as Conservative MP Michael Chong's Bill C-559 seeks to do. We can rebuild an independent expert and professional civil service and eliminate the contamination by political operatives. We can restore to Parliament the role of custodian and guardian of the public purse. We can insist that the federal budgets tabled in the House are actually budgets. We can restore the principles of Westminster parliamentary democracy by reversing the dangerous trends that have led to centralization of power.

We need to remind our members of parliament that under our Constitution they are elected to represent their constituents. I hope to be joined by more Green MPs so that we can prove this point by having Green MPs vote as they see fit. With two Green MPs in the House, Bruce Hyer and I are able to demonstrate that we can work together in one party without whipped votes. In the meantime, we need to encourage all MPs to speak up, to speak their minds, and to stop accepting the tyranny of political whiz kids and spin doctors who ply their craft in all the other parties. These unelected, unaccountable operatives are like leeches on the body politic. Some are my friends from other parties. They are pleasant and entertaining leeches. They have their place: during elections. Once a political campaign is over, they should be working in ad agencies or consulting firms, or even as baristas to improve their people skills.

What we have now is a nightmare of never-ending campaigning. Political posturing and hyper-partisan politicking have replaced policy making and good governance. We need the House of Commons to seek common ground and forge consensus. Wedge issues and momentary points scored against another party are completely unhelpful in the matter of governance.

And worse is the deliberate manipulation of citizens to vote against economic self-interest, to be manipulated through the distortions invented by the spin doctors to think that voting for ruthless individualism is some form of rebellion against elites.

The result is the increasing risk that politics has become a place of circuses and mob rule. Former MP Ken Dryden wrote of the degradation of politics and the celebration of the deliberate "know-nothings." He believes that both the Tea Party and Rob Ford are motivated by rage against the "know-everythings." In many ways, Dryden's analysis mirrors Laura Penny's "nerds versus bullies" narrative.

"They know something is wrong. They are mad as hell because they have every reason to be mad as hell. They can also make government seem even more useless," wrote Dryden.[2]

That may be our single biggest hurdle—believing that we can make government useful again. To solve the democracy crisis and the climate crisis, the public sphere must be resurrected as a legitimate space to get things done. As Naomi Klein has observed, "The reason that climate action is such a threat to neo-liberalism is that we need to re-invest in the commons immediately and on a huge scale."[3]

We will need to act deliberately and purposefully as citizens. As empowered citizens, we must reclaim our ability to limit market fundamentalism in the interests of survival while creating ideal conditions for healthy economic prosperity. It is not so much that the market cannot tell the truth; it is that without full costing, putting in markers for the externalities, markets are a rigged game. We will need to reclaim our collective goals of building the bridges and high-speed trains and infrastructure of a modern sustainable society.

One of my most loved friends, Farley Mowat, thought humanity was beyond redemption. He tried to persuade me that the planet will be better off without us. But I don't believe that. For one thing, by the time our species makes the planet uninhabitable for us, we will have condemned millions of other species to extinction. Sure, bacteria and roaches and micro-organisms that can exist in geothermal vents on the ocean floor should be fine, but the diverse, complex ecosystems that evolved over the last several million years will be toast. And even if, by some fluke, humanity could be snuffed while leaving flamingos, tortoises, and dolphins behind, I would mourn our loss.

We are not the only species worthy of consideration, but we are arguably the most interesting. We alone—of the ten million or so other species with whom we share this planet—have flirted with the creativity of the ultimate Creator, through our art, our music, our poetry. We know what it is to love, to laugh, to grieve. We are capable of making a decision in a nanosecond to sacrifice our life to save another. We are compassionate and empathetic and caring. Even the worst of us have some redeeming feature, somewhere. I love us. And I will not accept that we, the self-described smart ones—*homo sapiens*—are pathologically committed to stupidity.

Nevertheless, our intelligence can also be limiting. Our ability to develop models, allowing those models to stand as icons, can condemn us to being trapped in our cultural assumptions. We can be on the verge of systemic collapse, while noticing the wrong indicators of success. We can be locked in what Ron Wright describes as a "progress trap." Where technology has created risks, additional technologies are offered up as solutions, but they further compound the problem. It can all look fine on the surface, when, in fact, we are in dire peril.

Still, I sense something stirring. In the town hall meetings I hold in Saanich–Gulf Islands, citizens express a deep unease.

"Who owns this country?" asked one man. "Where has Canada gone?" asked a woman in another meeting. "I want my country back," is spoken over and over.

We need to wake up and smarten up. We do not lack solutions. We lack only the awareness of our situation, the courage to choose the right priorities (survival over short-term profits, life over money), and the political will to embrace them.

We are running out of time.

We need to get busy, rebuild our country, and start saving our own lives.

We need to remember who we are.

Notes

Introduction

1. David Korten, *The Post-Corporate World: Life after Capitalism* (San Francisco: Berrett-Koehler Publishing, 1999).

2. Bono, "Canada Liberal Party Convention-11/14/2003-Toronto, Ontario," Bono Speaks (blog), November 14, 2003, accessed April 29, 2014, http://bonospeaks.blogspot.ca/2003/11/canada-liberal-party-convention.html.

3. Victor Lebow, "Price Competition in 1955," *Journal of Retailing* (spring 1955).

Chapter 1

1. "June 9, 1954: Have You No Sense of Decency?" United States Senate, accessed April 30, 2014, http://www.senate.gov/artandhistory/history/minute/Have_you_no_sense_of_decency.htm.

2. Rachel Carson, *Silent Spring* (New York: Houghton Mifflin, 1962), 277.

3. Norton Juster, *The Phantom Tollbooth* (New York: Random House, 1961), 247.

Chapter 2

1. Legisinfo, Parliament of Canada, accessed May 8, 2014, http://www.parl.gc.ca/LegisInfo/Home.aspx?Language=E&Mode=1.

2. Brian Mulroney, "We Went from 'Yelling at the Rain,' to Talking Common Ground," *iPolitics,* March 14, 2012, accessed April 27, 2014, http://www.ipolitics.ca/2012/03/14/bian-mulroney-we-went-from-yelling-at-the-rain-to-talking-common-ground-acid-rain-treaty.

3. H.L. Ferguson, "The Changing Atmosphere: Implications for Global Security," in *The Challenge of Global Warming,* ed. Dean Abrahamson (Washington: Island Press, 1989), 44–62.

4. E.F. Schumacher, *Good Work* (New York: Harper & Row, 1979), 34–35.

Chapter 3

1. Paul Heinbecker, "A Conversation on Peace and Security" (speech, St. Paul's University, Ottawa, Canada, February 17, 2007).

2. William Clinton, Address (speech, Frank McKenna Annual Networking Event, Fox Harbour Golf Resort, July 27, 2007).

3. William Clinton, Address (speech, Conference of the Parties 11—United Nations Climate Change Conference, Montreal, Canada, December 8, 2005).

Chapter 4

1. Marilyn Waring, *If Women Counted: A New Feminist Economics* (San Francisco: Harper & Row, 1988).

2. Hazel Henderson, *The Politics of the Solar Age: Alternatives to Economics* (New York: Anchor Press/Doubleday, 1981), 181.

3. E.F. Schumacher, *Small Is Beautiful: A Study of Economics as if People Mattered* (New York: Harper & Row, 1973).

4. James Tobin, "Cooling Down Hot Money—Preventing the Next Financial Crisis" (speech, Ottawa, 1998).

5. John Kenneth Galbraith, *The Great Crash 1929* (New York: Houghton Mifflin, 1954), 98.

6. Naomi Klein, Address (speech, The Radical Emission Reduction Conference, London, Ontario, December 10, 2013).

7. Herman Daly, cited in Al Gore, *Our Choice* (New York: Rodale Press, 2009), 329.

8. Ernst von Weizsäcker, "The Old and New Europe: Alternatives for Future Transatlantic Relations?" (paper presented at Transatlantic Perspectives on Liberalization and Democratic Governance, Speyer, June 2003), accessed May 9, 2014, http://ernst.weizsaecker.de/en/the-old-and-new-europe-alternatives-for-future-transatlantic-relations/.

9. George Soros, "International Economic Turmoil," United States House of Representatives, September 15, 1998, accessed May 9, 2014, http://commdocs.house.gov/committees/bank/hba51202.000/hba51202_1.HTM.

10. Roger Cohen, "Capitalism Eating Its Children," *New York Times*, May 29, 2014.

11. Gaylord Nelson, cited in "A Former Senator Fights On," Nelson Institute for Environmental Studies, April 20, 2011, accessed May 12, 2014, http://www.nelsonearthday.net/nelson/fightingon.htm.

12. Peter Victor, *Managing without Growth—Slower by Design, Not Disaster* (Northampton: Edward Elgar Publishing, 2008).

13. Robert F. Kennedy Jr., "Crimes against Nature" (speech, St. Thomas University School of Law, February 2, 2006), accessed May 9, 2014, http://heinonline.org.

14. Benito Mussolini, cited in Kennedy.

15. Robert F. Kennedy, Address (speech, University of Kansas, Lawrence, Kansas, March 18, 1968).

16. P. Hawken, A. Lovins, and H. Lovins, *Natural Capitalism: The Next Industrial Revolution* (London: Earthscan, 1999), 261.

17. David Korten, *When Corporations Rule the World* (San Francisco: Berrett-Koehler Publishers, 2001), 249.

18. John Kenneth Galbraith, "Interview: Stop the Madness," *Globe and Mail*, July 6, 2002.

Chapter 5

1. Ronald Wright, letter to the editor, *Globe and Mail*, December 8, 2008.

2. Errol Mendes, "Jean's Decision Sets 'Very Dangerous' Precedent: Constitutional Expert," CBC *News*, December 4, 2008, accessed May 9, 2014, http://www.cbc.ca/m/touch/canada/story/1.706197.

3. Keith Spicer, "Zimbabwe Run by the Queen," *Ottawa Citizen*, December 15, 2008.

4. Andrew Coyne, "Andrew Coyne: U.S. and Canadian Political Systems Both Dysfunctional, in Opposing Ways," *National Post*, October 9, 2013. Used with permission of the author.

Chapter 6

1. Herbert Needleman et al., "Low-Level Environmental Lead Exposure and Children's Intellectual Function: An International Pooled Analysis," *Environmental Health Perspectives* 113, no. 7 (July 2005): 94–99, accessed May 9, 2014, doi: 10.1289/ehp.7688.

2. Gordon McBean, personal communication, February 15, 2014.

3. The Keeling Curve-Homepage, Scripps Institute of Oceanography, University of California San Diego, accessed April 27, 2014, http://keelingcurve.ucsd.edu.

4. Svante Arrhenius, "On the Influence of Carbonic Acid in the Air upon the Temperature of the Ground," *Philosophical Magazine and Journal of Science* 5, no. 41 (April 1896): 237–76.

5. Jean Baptiste Joseph Fourier, *Oeuvres de Fourier*, ed. Jean Gaston Darboux (Cambridge: Cambridge University Press, 2013).

6. Stephen Harper, cited in *Belief Revision Meets Philosophy of Science*, ed. Erik Olsson and Sebastian Enqvist (New York: Springer, 2011).

7. "Impact of the Kyoto Protocol on the Canadian Economy," Montreal Economic Institute, December 2, 2005, accessed May 11, 2014, http://www.iedm.org/uploaded/pdf/kyoto0106_en.pdf.

8. Gavin Schmidt, written correspondence with Ben Santer, December 2, 2008, accessed May 9, 2014, http://www.di2.nu/foia/1228258714.txt.

9. House of Commons Science and Technology Committee, "The Reviews into the University of East Anglia's Climatic Research Unit's E-mails," January 25, 2011, accessed May 11, 2014, http://www.publications.parliament.uk/pa/cm201011/cmselect/cmsctech/444/444.pdf.

10. "You Idiots! Meet The Planet's Worst Enemies: Inside The Battle Over Global Warming," *Rolling Stone,* January 21, 2010, 1096.

11. Daniel Tencer, "Koch Brothers, Tea Party Billionaires, Donated to Right-Wing Fraser Institute, Reports Show," *Huffington Post Canada,* April 26, 2012, accessed on June 12, 2014, http://www.huffingtonpost.ca/2012/04/26/koch-brothers-fraser-institute_n_1456223.html.

12. Steve Connor, "Exclusive: Billionaires Secretly Fund Attacks on Climate Science," *The Independent,* January 24, 2013, accessed May 11, 2014, http://www.independent.co.uk/environment/climate-change/exclusive-billionaires-secretly-fund-attacks-on-climate-science-8466312.html.

13. Ivan Semeniuk, "How Canada's Arctic Lab Keeps a Watchful Eye on Climate Change," *Globe and Mail,* January 21, 2014, accessed June 22, 2014, http://www.theglobeandmail.com/news/national/the-north/how-canadas-arctic-lab-keeps-a-watchful-eye-on-climate-change/article16423612/?page=all.

14. Peter Ross, cited in Cindy Harnett, "Killer Whale Expert Out of Work as Ottawa Cuts Ocean-Pollution Monitoring Positions," *National Post,* May 20, 2012, accessed May 11, 2014, http://news.nationalpost.com/2012/05/20/killer-whale-expert-out-of-work-as-ottawa-cuts-ocean-pollution-monitoring-positions.

15. Michael Harris, "The DFO and Science: A Fish Story," *iPolitics,* February 12, 2013, accessed May 11, 2014, http://www.ipolitics.ca/2013/02/12/the-dfo-and-science-a-fish-story.

16. Anonymous, "He Said, She Said... Who Is Lying?" *unmuz-zledscience*, February 10, 2013, accessed May 11, 2014, http://unmuzzledscience.wordpress.com/2013/02/10/he-said-she-said-who-is-lying.

17. Margaret Munro, "U.S. Scientist Rejects Ottawa's 'Muzzle,'" *Edmonton Journal*, February 14, 2013, accessed May 11, 2014, http://www2.canada.com/edmontonjournal/news/opinion/story.html?id=e29779a5-bec2-4c92-92cd-7615afb9a3a0.

18. Richard Kool, "In the Soviet Era as in Canada: Science Suffers under Authoritarian Rule," *Desmog Canada*, September 26, 2013, http://desmog.ca/2013/09/25/soviet-era-canada-science-suffers-under-authoritarian-rule. Used with permission of the author.

Chapter 7

1. James Hansen et al., "Climate Sensitivity, Sea Level and Atmospheric Carbon Dioxide," *Philosophical Transactions of the Royal Society A* 371, no. 2001 (October 2013), accessed May 11, 2104, http://rsta.royalsocietypublishing.org/content/371/2001/20120294.full.

2. Ahmed Nafeez, "James Hansen: Fossil Fuel Addiction Could Trigger Runaway Global Warming," *The Guardian*, July 10, 2013, accessed May 11, 2014, http://www.theguardian.com/environment/earth-insight/2013/jul/10/james-hansen-fossil-fuels-runaway-global-warming.

3. Donella H. Meadows, *The Limits to Growth* (New York: New American Library, 1972).

4. Julian Simon, *The Ultimate Resource* (Princeton: Princeton University Press, 1981).

5. Bjorn Lomborg, *The Skeptical Environmentalist: Measuring the Real State of the World*, trans. Hugh Matthews (Cambridge: Cambridge University Press, 2001), 106–8.

6. M. King Hubbert, "Energy from Fossil Fuels," *Science* 109 (February 4, 1949): 103–9, accessed May 11, 2014, http://www.hubbertpeak.com/hubbert/science1949.

7. Ajay Gupta and Charles Hall, "A Review of the Past and Current State of EROI Data," *Sustainability* 3, no. 10 (October 2011): 1796–1809, accessed May 11, 2014, http://www.mdpi.com/2071-1050/3/10/1796/htm.

8. Ed Struzik, "With Tar Sands Development, Growing Concern on Water Use," *Environment 360*, August 5, 2013, accessed May 11, 2104, http://e360.yale.edu/feature/with_tar_sands_development_growing_concern_on_water_use/2672.

9. Gupta and Hall.

10. Amory Lovins, "Negawatt Revolution," Rocky Mountain Institute, 1990, accessed May 11, 2014, http://www.rmi.org/Knowledge-Center/Library/E90-20_NegawattRevolution.

11. Kirstina Pistone, Ian Eisenman, and V. Ramanathan, "Observational Determination of Albedo Decrease Caused by Vanishing Arctic Sea Ice," *Proceedings of the National Academy of Sciences* 11, no. 9 (January 2014): 3322–26, accessed May 11, 2014, http://www.pnas.org/content/111/9/3322.short.

12. Andrew Nikiforuk, "Oh Canada: How America's Friendly Northern Neighbour Became a Rogue, Reckless Petro-State," *Foreign Policy*, June 24, 2013, accessed May 11, 2014, http://www.foreignpolicy.com/articles/2013/06/24/oh_canada.

13. Thomas Homer-Dixon, "The Tar Sands Disaster," *New York Times*, March 31, 2013, accessed May 11, 2014, http://www.nytimes.com/2013/04/01/opinion/the-tar-sands-disaster.html?_r=0.

14. Thomas Friedman, "The First Law of Petropolitics," *Foreign Policy*, April 25, 2006, accessed May 11, 2014, http://www.foreignpolicy.com/articles/2006/04/25/the_first_law_of_petropolitics.

15. Ishmael Daro, "All Norwegians Are Millionaires Now. That Must Be Nice," *The Albatross*, January 10, 2014, accessed May 11, 2014,

http://www.thealbatross.ca/27592/all-norwegians-are-millionaires-now.

16. William Marsden, *Stupid to the Last Drop: How Alberta Is Bringing Environmental Armageddon to Canada (and Doesn't Seem to Care)* (Toronto: Knopf Canada, 2007).

17. Organisation for Economic Co-operation and Development, "OECD Economic Surveys: Canada 2008," OECD Publishing, July 2, 2008.

18. Statistics Canada, "Table 379-0031—Gross Domestic Product (GDP) at Basic Prices, by North American Industry Classification System (NAICS), Monthly (Dollars), CANSIM (Database)," accessed May 12, 2014, http://www5.statcan.gc.ca/cansim/a26?lang=eng&id=3790031&p2=17.

19. Nikiforuk.

20. Laura Penny, *More Money than Brains* (New York: McClelland & Stewart, 2010), 7, 233.

Chapter 8

1. Petra Kelly, *Non-Violence Speaks to Power*, ed. Glenn D. Paige and Sarah Gilliatt (Honolulu: Center for Non-Violence, 2001), 28.

2. David W. Orr, *Down to the Wire: Confronting Climate Collapse* (New York: Oxford University Press, 2009), 14.

3. Mary Fagan, "Sheik Yamani Predicts Price Crash as Age of Oil Ends," *The Telegraph*, June 25, 2000, accessed May 11, 2014, http://www.telegraph.co.uk/news/uknews/1344832/Sheikh-Yamani-predicts-price-crash-as-age-of-oil-ends.html.

4. Bob Salsberg and Steve Leblanc, "Gomez, Markey Spar in 2nd Senate Debate," *The Telegram*, June 11, 2013, accessed May 11, 2014, http://www.telegram.com/article/20130611/NEWS/306119608/1116.

5. Dan Woynillowicz, Penelope Comette, and Ed Whittingham, "Competing in Clean Energy: Capitalizing on Canadian Innovation

in a $3 Trillion Economy," Pembina Institute, January 22, 2013, accessed May 11, 2014, http://www.pembina.org/pub/2406.

6. Ralph Torrie, "Kyoto and Beyond: The Low Emission Path to Innovation and Efficiency," David Suzuki Foundation; Climate Action Network, September 2002, 22–23, accessed May 11, 2014, http://www.davidsuzuki.org/publications/downloads/2002/Kyoto_Beyond_eng.pdf.

7. Mark Jaccard, "The Climate Change Olympics: Perhaps Some Healthy Provincial Competition Can Get Canada Moving," *The Literary Review of Canada,* May 2010, accessed May 11, 2014, http://reviewcanada.ca/magazine/2010/05/the-climate-change-olympics.

8. Bill Moyers, "This Isn't the Speech I Expected to Give Today" (speech, Environmental Grantmakers Association, Brainerd, Minnesota, October 16, 2001), accessed May 11, 2014, https://www.commondreams.org/views01/1030-07.htm.

Chapter 9

1. Stephen Harper, cited in "Harper Questions Claim of Deliberate Attack," Canwest News Service, Canada.com, July 27, 2006, accessed May 11, 2014, http://www.canada.com/nationalpost/story.html?id=e6382a3c-8c85-4232-ba6b-f6cd9b09a44c.

2. "Tories Defend Withdrawal from UN Drought 'Talkfest,'" *CBC News,* March 28, 2013, accessed May 11, 2014, http://www.cbc.ca/news/politics/tories-defend-withdrawal-from-un-drought-talkfest-1.1317593.

3. Ibid.

4. Eric Reguly, "Canada's $207,000 Oil Sands Ad: Putting a Price on Deception," *Globe and Mail,* May 9, 2014, p. 1.

5. Harrison Samphir, "Dropping UN Drought Convention: The Death Knell of Canada's International Reputation?" *Rabble.ca,* April 3, 2013, accessed May 11, 2014, http://rabble.ca/news/2013/04/dropping-un-drought-convention-death-knell-canadas-international-reputation.

6. Joseph de Maistre, *Lettres et Opuscules Inédits,* vol. 1, letter 53, August 15, 1811, published in 1851.

7. Joe Clark, *How We Lead: Canada in a Century of Change* (Toronto: Random House Canada, 2013).

8. Arthur Black, Address (speech, Oh Canada... Stand on Guard, Vernon, British Columbia, April 8, 2013).

9. Alan Ryan, *On Politics: A History of Political Thought from Herodotus to the Present* (New York: W.W. Norton, 2012), 95.

10. Petra Kelly, *Fighting for Hope* (New York: South End Press, 1984), 17.

11. Tom Robbins, *Still Life with Woodpecker* (New York: Bantam Books, 1980), 92.

12. Aldous Huxley, *Brave New World* (London: Chatto & Windus, 1932), 244.

Chapter 10

1. Christopher Waddell and David Taras, *How Canadians Communicate IV: Media and Politics* (Edmonton: Athabasca University Press, 2012).

2. Ken Dryden, "Why Rob Ford Is Mad as Hell," *Globe and Mail,* December 19, 2013.

3. Naomi Klein, Address (speech, The Radical Emission Reduction Conference, London, Ontario, December 10, 2013).

Other Books by Elizabeth May

*Losing Confidence: Power, Politics and the Crisis
in Canadian Democracy*
(Toronto: MCCLELLAND AND STEWART, 2009)

With Zoe Caron. *Global Warming for Dummies*
(Toronto: JOHN WILEY AND SONS, 2008)

How to Save the World in Your Spare Time
(Toronto: KEY PORTER BOOKS, 2006)

*At the Cutting Edge—The Crisis in Canada's Forests:
Revised and Expanded*
(Toronto: KEY PORTER BOOKS, 2005)

With Maude Barlow. *Frederick Street—Life and
Death on Canada's Love Canal*
(Toronto: HARPERCOLLINS, 2000)

At the Cutting Edge—The Crisis in Canada's Forests
(Toronto: KEY PORTER BOOKS, 1998)

Paradise Won—The Struggle for South Moresby
(Toronto: MCCLELLAND AND STEWART, 1990)

Budworm Battles
(Tantallon, NS: FOUR EAST PUBLICATIONS, 1982)